Use It! Don't Lose It!

MATH
Daily Skills Practice
Grade 7

by Marjorie Frank

IncentivePublications

Illustrated by Kathleen Bullock
Cover by Geoffrey Brittingham
Edited by Jill Norris
Copy-edited by Cary Grayson and Steve Carlon

ISBN 978-0-86530-666-0

7   8   9   10   13   12   11

Printed by Sheridan Books, Inc., Chelsea, Michigan • January 2011
www.incentivepublications.com

Don't let those math skills get lost or rusty!

As a teacher you work hard to teach math skills to your students. Your students work hard to master them. Do you worry that your students will forget the material as you move on to the next concept?

If so, here's a plan for you and your students—one that will keep those skills sharp.

Use It! Don't Lose It! provides daily math practice for all the basic skills. There are five math problems a day, every day for 36 weeks. The skills are correlated to national and state standards.

Students practice all the seventh-grade skills, concepts, and processes in a spiraling sequence. The plan starts with the simplest level of seventh-grade skills, progressing gradually to higher-level tasks, as it continually circles around and back to the the same skills at a little higher level, again and again. Each time a skill shows up, it has a new context—requiring students to dig into their memories, recall what they know, and apply it to another situation.

The Weekly Plan — Five Problems a Day for 36 Weeks

Monday – Thursday .... • one computation item
  Monday – whole numbers   Wednesday – integers
  Tuesday – decimals   Thursday – fractions
  • one problem-solving task (word problem)
  • one algebra item

Monday and **Wednesday** .... • one statistics or probability item
  • one geometry item

Tuesday and **Thursday** .... • one measurement item
  • one number concepts item

Friday .... • two computation items
  • one algebra item
  • one item rotating among math strands
  • one *Challenge Problem* demanding more involved
    steps, thinking skills, and calculations
    (making use of several skills)

Contents

How to Use Daily Skills Practice

To get started, reproduce each page, slice the Monday–Thursday lesson pages in half, or prepare a transparency. The lessons can be used . . .

- **for independent practice**—Reproduce the lessons and let students work individually or in pairs to practice skills at the beginning or end of a math class.
- **for small group work**—Students can discuss and solve the problems together and agree on answers.
- **for the whole class review**—Make a transparency and work through the problems together as a class.

Helpful Hints for Getting Started

- Though students may work alone on the items, always find a way to review and discuss the answers together. In each review, ask students to describe how they solved the problem-solving problems or other problems that involve choices of strategies.

- Allow more time for the Friday lesson. The Challenge Problem may take a little longer. Students can work in small groups to discover good strategies and correct answers for this problem.

- Provide measurement tools and other supplies students need for solving the problems. There will not be room on the sheet for all problems to be solved. Students will need scratch paper for their work.

- Decide ahead of time about the use of calculators. Since the emphasis is on students practicing their skills, it is recommended that the items be done without calculators and other calculation aids. If you want to focus specifically on technology skills, set a particular goal for certain lessons to be done or checked with calculators. You might allow calculator use for the Friday Challenge Problems.

- The daily lessons are designed to be completed in a short time period, so that they can be used along with your regular daily instruction. However, don't end the discussion until you are sure all students "get it," or at least until you know which ones don't get something and will need extra instruction. This will strengthen all the other work students do in math class.

- Keep a consistent focus on the strategies and processes for problem solving. Encourage students to explore and share different approaches for solving the problems. Explaining (orally or in writing) their problem-solving process is an important math skill. Be open to answers (correct ones, of course) that are not supplied in the Answer Key.

- Take note of which items leave some or all of the students confused or uncertain. This will alert you to which skills need more instruction.

- The daily lessons may include some topics or skills your students have not yet learned. In these cases, students may skip items. Or, you might encourage them to consider how the problem could be solved. Or, you might use the occasion for a short lesson that would get them started on this skill.

1. Compute: **986**
+ 175

2. Give the rule for the number sequence.
Write the next three numbers.

1, 3, 8, 19, 42, 89, ____, ____, ____

3. In a set of data, the sum of the data
divided by the number of data items is the

○ range   ○ median
○ mean   ○ mode

4. Draw a pair of perpendicular lines.

I'm famous.

5. Can this problem be solved with the
information given?

In 1933, a London circus
offered a reward in the amount
of 20,000 British pounds for the
capture of the Loch Ness
Monster. In 2005, a professor
from Maine announced a
$1 million reward for a
photograph of the Loch Ness
Monster, Bigfoot, or the
Abominable Snowman that
would lead to the capture of any
one of the three legendary
creatures. What is the difference
between the amounts of the
two rewards?

1. Which statement is **not** true?

a. A composite number can be divided by two.

b. –2.5 is an integer.

c. A fraction is a rational number.

d. An integer is a counting number.

2. Write this number in standard notation:

sixty-six thousand, sixty-six

3. Compute: **4.94 + 0.02**

4. Which units are metric units?

○ grams   ○ liters   ○ yards   ○ ounces

○ inches   ○ kilometers   ○ acres   ○ meters

5. What information is **not** needed to
solve the problem?

In the mountains of Nepal, some
climbers found footprints at an
altitude of 18,000 feet. The
footprints measured 11 inches long
and 5 inches wide. Other climbers
claim that they saw a Yeti in the
same area at 16,595 feet. What is
the difference in the elevations at
which the two sightings occurred?

Yodel – yeti – ooo!

WEDNESDAY WEEK 1 _____ MATH PRACTICE
Name

1. What operation is needed to solve the problem?

> Sailors insisted that the Kraken (a large sea creature) was 1,700 feet in diameter when its tentacles were outstretched. About what would the circumference of this creature be?

2.

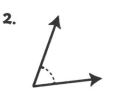

This angle is a(n) _____ angle.

3. What number is the opposite of **–37**?

4. Compute: **–16 + 8 =**

5. Which three-month period had the most sightings of all three creatures?

Creature Sightings

Month	Bigfoot	Nessie	Yeti
Jan	13	16	9
Feb	10	22	3
Mar	24	7	4
Apr	33	5	6
May	35	23	8
Jun	47	50	18
July	37	37	28
Aug	40	35	27
Sept	35	20	4
Oct	18	26	2
Nov	6	18	0
Dec	4	12	0

THURSDAY WEEK 1 _____ MATH PRACTICE
Name

1. What is the absolute value of **–135**?

2. Compute: $\frac{3}{8} + \frac{1}{8} + \frac{3}{8} =$

3. Put these in order from least to greatest:

2,022	22
220	20,200
2,202	202

4. If an average of 1,135 visitors go to Scotland's Loch Ness each month, how many people visit in one year?

5. a. Measure the footprint in centimeters. *(Round to the nearest centimeter.)*

b. If the scale of the drawing is *1 cm = 2 in,* how big would the actual footprint be?

Oh, my!

Name

1. Compute: (−16) − 20 =

2. Compute: 345
                    x 27

3. Which expression matches the words?

twice the difference between twelve and a number

  a. **2n − 12**
  b. **2(12 − n)**
  c. **2(n − 12)**
  d. **2 x 12 − n**

4. Which event has the **least** likelihood of happening?

  a. Evening will come today.

  b. You choose the name of a weekday and get a day beginning with T.

  c. A bubblegum machine has 100 green and 10 yellow gumballs. You put in a coin and get a yellow gumball.

  d. You flip a coin and it lands tails up.

5. Challenge Problem

Three friends liked to track down legendary creatures. The diagram shows some statistics on what they saw in a three-year period of searching.

  a. Which friend had the most sightings?

  b. Which friend saw only two of the three creatures (or footprints)?

  c. Which creature (or prints) was seen the most times?

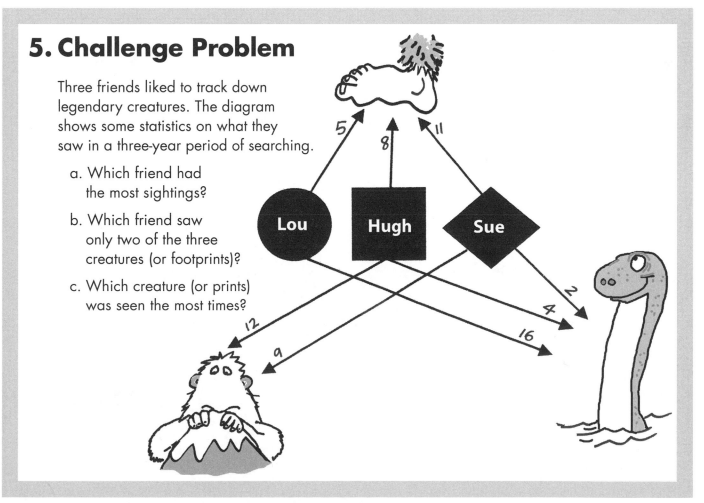

1. Estimate the solution.

The average thickness of the ice cap over the South Pole is the nine times the height of the Eiffel Tower. The Eiffel Tower is 1,052 feet tall. About how thick is the ice cap?

2. Which expression matches the words?

three times the square of a number (n)

a. $3n^2$ b. n^3 c. $3 + n^2$ d. $3^2 + n$

3. Compute: 17,963
                   – 1,298

4. The name of each month is written once on a slip of paper and put into a bag. Without looking, you choose one slip. What are the possible outcomes?

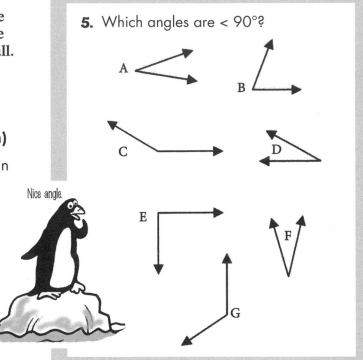

5. Which angles are < 90°?

A

B

C

D

E

F

G

Nice angle.

1. What is the value of the digit **6** in the number?

33,602,541

I should know this.

2. How many **terms** are in this expression?

34 + 2x – x

3. Compute: **5.2 x 0.3 =**

4. Which of these is the best unit for measuring the height of an iceberg?

○ inches   ○ square centimeters

○ meters   ○ kilometers

○ millimeters   ○ square kilometers

5. What operations are needed to solve this problem?

Some 20 to 30 million tons of ice break off the Jakobshavn Glacier in Greenland every day, forming icebergs. Approximately how many pounds of icebergs break off from the glacier in an hour?

Row, row, row your iceberg
Gently down the stream...

8

1. In the year 2000, a huge iceberg broke off the Ross Ice Shelf in Antarctica. Possibly the largest iceberg ever, it measured 783 miles long and 23 miles wide. What was the area of its top surface?

2. Name this figure.

3. What is the **variable** in this expression?

$$300 - 25b + b$$

4. Compute: $-5 \times 12 =$

5. About what percent of Earth's surface is covered with water?

Earth's Land, Water, and Ice

1. What is the value of **n**?

$$400n = 0$$

2. Compute: $\frac{1}{2} \times \frac{2}{3}$

3. Wes and Leslie create an ice rink by spraying water on an area that is 28 feet by 21 feet. The ice is 6 inches thick. Estimate the volume of the ice in their rink.

4. Round **37,406** to the nearest ten.

5. Louisa is monitoring the melting of ten different glaciers. She has compiled data about the number of feet each of the glaciers has receded each month for the past six months. Now, she's ready to find out which glaciers had the most and the least melting.

Which strategy is best to help solve this problem?

    a. Draw a diagram.

    b. Use trial and error.

    c. Create a table.

    d. Translate the problem into an equation.

1. Compute:

$$-\frac{2}{8} + \frac{1}{4} + \frac{1}{3} =$$

2. Which demonstrates the **commutative property for multiplication**?

   a. $3(a + b) = 3a + 3b$

   b. $25 + 6 = 6 + 25$

   c. $8 \times (4 \times 7) = (8 \times 4) \times 7$

   d. $35 \times 12 = 12 \times 35$

3. In the following equation, what is the **coefficient** of the variable?

$$5 + 100n - 15 = 390$$

4. What is the **mean** of this set of data?

23 ft	**8 ft**	**7 ft**
12 ft	**3 ft**	**8 ft**
16 ft	**11 ft**	**20 ft**

5. Challenge Problem

Tyson wants to paddle his kayak around the outside edge of each iceberg to see all sides. He can paddle about 12 miles an hour. Estimate the amount of time it will take him to get around each iceberg.

A. The part of this glacier above water is almost a perfect **cube.**

B. The part of this glacier above water is **cone-shaped.**

C. The part of this glacier above water is shaped like a **rectangular prism.**

1. Rewrite the equation using the inverse operation.

$$32 \times 68 = 2176$$

2. Any segment that has both endpoints on a circle's circumference is a(n)

    a. diameter

    b. chord

    c. tangent

    d. central angle

3. Write the expression to match the words:

the sum of ten times a number (x) and five

I ran 10 times the number of days that the other sneakers ran, plus five more!

4. List all the possible outcomes for the random selection of the name of a month with 30 days.

5. Before a bodybuilding competition, Sabrina piled up a plate with 83 ounces of pasta. She ate 75 percent of it in nine minutes.

Use only mental math to estimate . . .

    a. how much pasta she ate.

    b. how much she ate per minute.

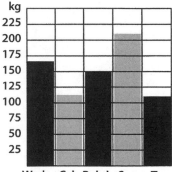

Maybe it's time for a spaghetti break?

1. Compute:

$$23.08 - 7.26 =$$

2. Circle the prime numbers.

    3   14   19   24

    25   29   31

3. Fill in the missing integer.

$$-10 + 8 + \underline{\hspace{1cm}} = -20$$

4. Which angles are obtuse?

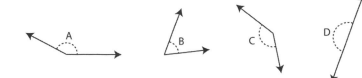

5. Which athlete lifted about ten percent more than Ralph?

Oakdale Lifting Competition

Wade   Cal   Ralph   Sam   Ty

1. A negative number divided by a negative number yields a

    a. positive number

    b. negative number

2. Is this reasonable?

   Jessica's weightlifting team drinks plenty of water during the hour that follows a competition. There are nine team members. One team member estimates that they drank 12 kiloliters after yesterday's competition.

Whew!

3. Compute: $-25 \div 5 =$

4. Rosa wants to show the time she has spent training each month for the last year. The best way to do this is with a

    a. line graph   c. double bar graph

    b. circle graph   d. pictograph

5. Which figures are symmetrical?

1001

1. Use words to write this expression: $\dfrac{d}{10}$

2. Convert the measurement of the weight Max just lifted.

   122,000 g = _____ kg

I wish I could do math in my head.

3. Compute: $\dfrac{1}{3} \div \dfrac{3}{4} =$

4. Which are *common multiples* of **4** and **7**?

    24   28   56   70

    42   84   91   112

5. Set up a proportion that could be used to solve this problem.

   Greg took first place in eight out of the last fifteen bodybuilding competitions he entered. At this rate, how many contests will he need to enter to win forty?

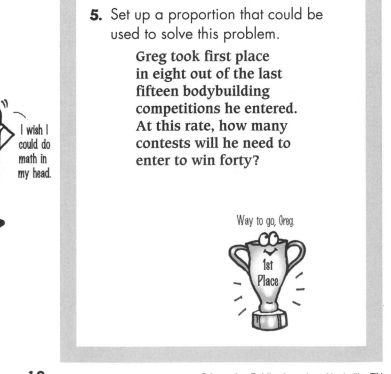

Way to go, Greg.

1st Place

1. Estimate the solution:

$$182 - 97 + 41 =$$

2. Find the average of these numbers.

42, 120, 75, 64, 93, 86

3. What are the **common factors** of **63** and **42**?

4. Which equation matches the words?

The sum of fifty-four and a number squared is seventy.

a. $54 + n = 70$
b. $54 + 70 = n^2$
c. $54 + n^2 = 70$
d. $70 - n^2 = 54$

5. Challenge Problem

Weightlifters on Lulu's team have made some calculations about their statistics. Examine their answers and conclusions to find out if they have calculated accurately. Give a **yes** or **no** answer for each item. If the calculation is wrong, give the correct answer.

Calculations:

a. The average age is 26.

b. Our average body weight is 59 kg.

c. The team member who started weightlifting at the youngest age is Lulu.

d. The average weight lifted is 156 kg.

e. The person who has 16 fewer years of experience than Maria is Simone.

f. The person whose best lift is about 40 kg less than Lulu's is Simone.

Simone
Age: *21*
Body Weight: *63 kg*
Years Weightlifting: *2000-2005*
Record Weight Lifted: *141kg*

Lulu
Age: *18*
Body Weight: *55 kg*
Years Weightlifting: *1998-2005*
Record Weight Lifted: *183.5 kg*

Bernadette
Age: *31*
Body Weight: *60 kg*
Years Weightlifting: *1996-2002*
Record Weight Lifted: *124.5 kg*

Maria
Age: *34*
Body Weight: *50 kg*
Years Weightifting: *1982-2003*
Record Weight Lifted: *175 kg*

1. The pirate schooner moved quietly through the water at 11 knots. (A knot is about 1.15 miles per hour.) How fast (in mph) did the schooner move?

2. Compute: **420 x 300 =**

3. The product of **–7** and **60** is

    a. –67   c. –420

    b. 420   d. 53

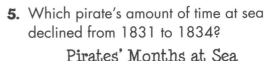

We've been at sea for a long time.

4. Which transformation is shown here?

    a. slide   b. flip   c. turn

5. Which pirate's amount of time at sea declined from 1831 to 1834?

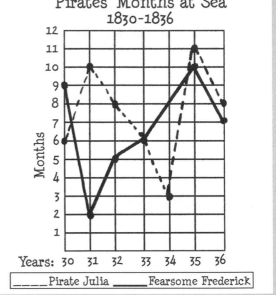

Pirates' Months at Sea
1830–1836

Months (y-axis: 1–12)

Years: 30 31 32 33 34 35 36

_____Pirate Julia _____Fearsome Frederick

1. Compute: $2.3\overline{)7.36}$

2. Which metric measure is closest to 30 gallons?

    a. 1200 mL   c. 300 g

    b. 120 L   d. 300cm³

3. What are the *like terms* in this equation?

    8n + 5b – 2n + 16 = 50

4. Is this statement true or false?

The following numbers are divisible by 4: 240, 72, 28, 108, 84, and 256

Avast, me hearties, it looks like we're headed for a collision!

5. Use trial and error to find the solution to the problem.

Two pirate ships are headed toward each other. They are 600 miles apart. The Green Dragon is traveling eastward at about 10 mph. The Black Serpent is traveling westward at about 12 mph. If the winds do not interfere with the progress of either ship, about how long will it be before they meet?

1. Which has the greater absolute value:
–300 or **288**?

2. Compute: **12 + –6 – (–3) =**

3. Translate the problem into an
equation and find a solution.

**Two pirates counted their gold
coins. Pirate Thomas had three
times as many as Pirate Jack.
Together they had 18,500.
How many coins did Jack have?**

*Pirate's treasure
here.*

4. Give the name of the space figures
below that have five faces.

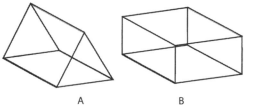

     A   B   C

5. Someone spins this spinner one time.
What is the probability that the
spinner will stop on a section other
than *treasure chest*?

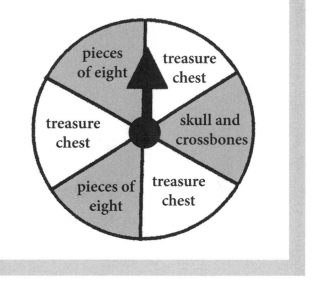

1. Ashleigh read the stories of 75 different
pirates. She says that four percent of them
were women. How many women pirates
were a part of Ashleigh's reading?

2. Write an expression to match the words:

**the difference between a number
(y) and twice another number (x)**

3. The value of **5⁴** is _____

4. Finish the number sentence to show the
commutative property of addition.

$$\frac{5}{9} + \frac{2}{3} =$$

5. Which is greater: the **perimeter**
of the flag or the **circumference** of
the cannon's mouth?

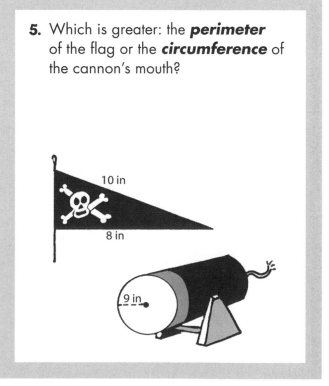

1. Is this answer correct?

$$\frac{3}{8} \div \frac{3}{4} = \frac{1}{2}$$

2. Which operation should be done first when solving the following equation?

$$6(5 + 2) - x =$$

3. Simplify the expression.

$$16 + 12b + 3b - 4$$

4. Find the area of this figure.

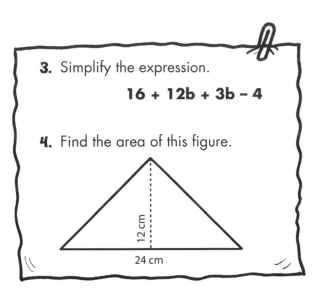

12 cm

24 cm

5. Challenge Problem

Pirate Victor Vile was a nasty villain. Few people have any good memories of him. It seems, however, that mean old Victor had a soft heart where his pet parrot, Pete, was concerned. When Pete disappeared, Pirate Victor became glum. As the days and weeks wore on, Victor's mood grew more and more glum. To the relief of the crew, Pete miraculously reappeared—just when they thought they could bear Victor's malaise no longer. Solve the problem to find out when the parrot returned.

I'm not really lost.

- Pete disappeared on the morning of September 28, 1815.

- For 95 days, Victor sailed to all the islands in the area, searching each one thoroughly.

- On the 96th day, Victor began sailing back and forth across the sea, stopping every ship, scouring it from top to bottom. He did this for exactly five weeks.

- The next morning, Victor went below deck and locked himself in his cabin for 35 days.

- On the 36th day, a storm rocked the boat so badly that Victor had to come up on deck.

- Just as the storm quieted, Victor heard a familiar voice saying, "Pretty bad pirate. Pretty bad pirate." You can imagine the jig they danced around the deck that day!

What was the date?

Name

1. A car named *Thrust SSC* set the record for the fastest land speed ever for one mile. *Thrust's* speed was 763.005 mph. About how long did it take the car to go the mile?

   a. 13 min

   b. 0.08 min

   c. 0.8 min

2. Compute: $61 \overline{)5,246}$

3. Simplify the expression:

   26g + 30 + 5g − 7

4. A quadrilateral has only two parallel sides. What is it?

Start your engines.

5. Which vehicle set its record traveling about 80 mph faster than the pickup truck?

SPEED RECORDS

vehicle	record speed (mph)	year
fastest electric car	245.951	*1999*
fastest steam car	145.607	*1985*
fastest diesel engine car	235.756	*1973*
fastest pickup truck	154.587	*2004*

Name

1. Joe wins a prize in a soapbox derby. He gets to choose one of eight envelopes. Five of the envelopes have $200. The other three hold $500. What are the odds in favor of Joe getting $500?

2. Compute: **$46.23 x 2 =**

3. Write this number in words: **204,310**

4. Charlene buys a new tire for her racecar. She flops it down on her garage floor. What area does it cover?

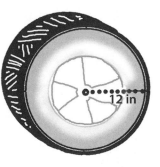

12 in

5. Choose the equation to correctly solve the problem .

   The stands at the Talladega Superspeedway hold 143,000 spectators. Five companies bought blocks of seats totaling half the seats. Each of four companies bought the same number of seats. The fifth company bought twice as many as the others combined. How many seats did the companies with an equal number of seats buy?

   ○ **4s + 2(4s) = 143,000**

   ○ **4s + 2(4s) = 71,500**

   ○ **5s = 71,500**

   ○ **12s = 143,000**

1. Christina went to a soap box derby race with 12 coins in her pocket. They totaled $1.20. What could these coins be? Give three different answers.

2. Write words to match the expression:

$$5p \div 2 =$$

3. Angela tosses a coin. Then she draws the name of a day of the week from a box. (The box holds seven slips of paper, each with the name of one of the days.) List all the possible outcomes of these events.

4. Compute:
$$-25 + 40 + 5 - (-20) =$$

5. Which figures are similar to the one without a letter?

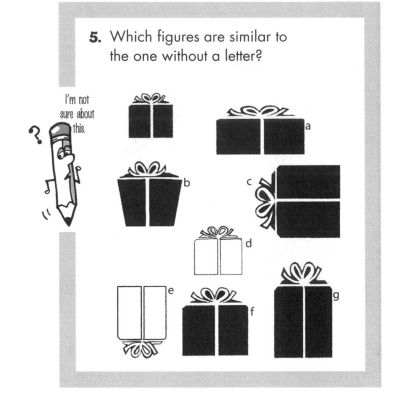

I'm not sure about this.

1. Which measurement statements are reasonable?
   a. A racehorse runs 60 k/hr.
   b. A bathtub holds 100 L of water.
   c. A car steering wheel is 20 m wide.
   d. A racecar weighs 800 kg.

2. Compute: $\dfrac{7}{3} \times \dfrac{5}{6} =$

No problem!

3. Which number is nine hundred ninety and ninety-nine thousandths?
   a. 909.099
   b. 990.99
   c. 990.099

4. Describe and finish the pattern.

   100, 80, 90, 70, 80, 60, ___, ___, ___

5. Will is fixing up his racecar. He needs some paint that costs $36.00 and some replacement parts that cost $197.65. His state charges eight percent sales tax. Will has 38 five-dollar bills, 4 ten-dollar bills, and 100 quarters.
Does he have enough to buy the supplies he wants?

I hope he has enough.

1. How many faces are there on a

    a. cube

    b. sphere

    c. cone

    d. cylinder

2. Compute: **362 x 143 =**

    a. 32,166

    b. 51,766

    c. 51,776

    d. 52,776

3. Fill in the missing operation.

$$0.6 \;\boxed{}\; 32.05 = 19.23$$

4. Write an equation that can be used to solve the problem. Solve the problem.

The Larson family drove to Baja for the *Baja 1000* race. In Baja, they met up with Grandma and Grandpa Larson, who drove from another location. Together, the two parts of the family traveled 2,100 miles. The younger Larsons drove 250 miles fewer than Grandma and Grandpa. How far did Grandma and Grandpa drive?

5. Challenge Problem

The clues give some information about how the five racers are doing in the soapbox derby. Combine good logical thinking with the diagram to figure out where each driver currently places.

Clues

Fran is **ahead** of Stan and Nan.

Van is **ahead** of Nan.

Nan is just **behind** Fran.

Dan is **behind** Nan.

Van is **ahead** of Stan.

Fran is just **behind** Van.

1. Simplify the expression:

$$\frac{18b}{3}$$

2. Write an addition problem with integers to solve this problem.

> **Sue took good care of her meat-eating plant. It grew from a seed to a six-inches tall plant in three weeks. Then she forgot to water it. The plant lost two inches in height. How tall was the plant then?**

Someone has shrunk.

3. Compute: $113\overline{)2{,}599}$

4. Define a **line segment**. Draw one.

5. Finish the tree diagram to show the possible outcomes of the two events: grabbing a piece of candy from a bag that has one of each (cherry, lime, grape), and drawing a bill from a box that has an equal number of $50s, $20s, and $10s.

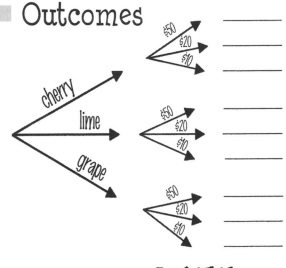

Outcomes

cherry — $50, $20, $10 — _____ _____ _____

lime — $50, $20, $10 — _____ _____ _____

grape — $50, $20, $10 — _____ _____ _____

1. Fill in the missing symbol: **<, >,** or **=**

35.505 ☐ **35.55**

2. Show three other ways to represent the value of this number. Use words, numerals, and/or symbols.

0.25

3. Compute:

4.362 x 3.1 =

4. Find the area of this figure.

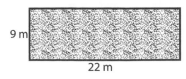

9 m

22 m

5. What information in the problem is NOT needed in order to find a solution?

> **There are 450 different kinds of meat-eating plants. Sue has photographed 28 percent of them. She has seven photos of a Venus's flytrap plant and ten photos of a sundew plant. She spent three months searching for a pitcher plant, and finally took five photos. How many different meat-eating plants has Sue photographed?**

CHEESE!

1. Write this equation:

   Six times the square of a number equals ninety-six

   Figure it out.

2. Compute: **12 x −4 =**

3. The difference between the greatest and least values in a set of data is the

   ○ mean   ○ range

   ○ median   ○ frequency

4. Is **200,000** a reasonable solution to this problem?

   A basket starfish has 50 arms. Frank mistakenly caught 35 of these animals in a basket. How many starfish arms were in that basket?

   Some of these starfish arms are sharp.

5. Which figure is congruent to the first one?

   a

   b

   c

   d

1. Give the place value for each **4** in the following number.

   404,243,040

2. What is the *coefficient* in the equation?

   $$\frac{10x}{3} = 200$$

3. Compute: $7\frac{7}{9} - 3\frac{2}{3} =$

4. The bombardier beetle defends itself by squirting a hot liquid on its enemies. This liquid is the temperature of boiling water. It could be

   ○ 100° F   ○ 100° C   ○ 33° C

   ○ 212° F   ○ 180° F   ○ 212° C

5. Michelle has kept a record of the odd birds she's spotted over the past three years. In which year did she see the fewest of these birds?

Odd Bird Sightings

Bird	sightings in 2003	sightings in 2004	sightings in 2005
ostriches	27	29	32
flamingos	47	60	22
vultures	6	9	8
spoonbills	5	17	1
turkeys	7	19	29

Name

1. Estimate the answer

$$31.2 + 19.9 + 146 - 52 =$$

3. Compute:

$$22 - \frac{9+3}{6} =$$

4. $2w + y = 6$

   a. Find **y** if **w** = –4.

   b. Find **y** if **w** = 10.

2. There are 60 gumballs in a machine: 30 blue, 10 red, and 20 yellow. Lucy puts in a quarter and gets a red gumball. She puts in a second quarter. She wonders, "What is the probability that I will get another red gumball?"

Lucy is getting two gumballs. Are these independent or dependent events? Explain your answer.

5. Challenge Problem

   a. Identify and describe the first pattern. Continue the pattern by drawing the next three plants in the space below the top row of plants.

   b. Identify and describe the second pattern. Continue the pattern by drawing the next three sets of items to follow the pattern.

Name

1. Brad has 80 books by the great mystery writer, Agatha Christie. He wants to read them all in a year. If he reads 25 percent of a book every day, will he finish all 80 in one year?

2. Which statements are true?

    a. All quadrilaterals have four sides.

    b. A rectangle is a rhombus.

    c. All rectangles have four right angles.

    d. All parallelograms are rectangles.

3. Simplify the equation.

$$35x + 12 - 18 = 64$$

4. Use the inverse operation to check the accuracy of this answer.

$$23 \times 42 = 966$$

5. Give the coordinates of all the footprints.

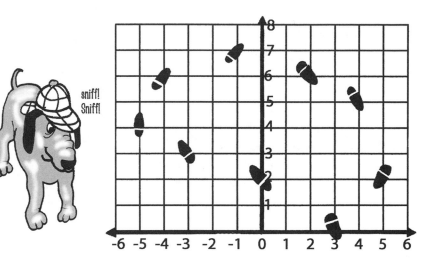

sniff!
Sniff!

Name

1. Put these in order from least to greatest.

    1.6   6.06   0.66

    1.066   6.006

2. A(n) _____ number is a number that can be written as a quotient of two integers.

3. Compute: $7 \overline{)3.003}$

4. Measure the thumbprint in centimeters. Round to the nearest centimeter.

5. Find the pattern to predict the total number of cases that will come to the agency in July, August, and September.

Sure-Fire Detective Agency Cases January – June

Month	Robberies	Disappearances	Other
Jan	22	24	8
Feb	26	30	4
Mar	35	25	8
Apr	30	26	22
May	12	42	36
June	47	16	41

1. Compute: $-4\overline{)1,120}$

2. The sum measurements of angles in a parallelogram is _____.

3. Solve the equation:

$$k - 23 = 50$$

4. Temperatures were so cold on the night of the robbery that no footprints were left at the scene. At 7 p.m., the temperature was 14° F. By midnight, the temperature had fallen to –6° F. Will this problem help find the difference between the two temperatures?

$$14 - (-6) = \text{_____}$$

I see a clue!

5. Detective Sally I. Gaucha finds some clues at the scene of a burglary. Find the probabilities connected to the clues.

  a. She finds a fingerprint. What is the probability that it is a print of an index finger?

  b. Sally finds some DNA on a lollipop stick. What is the probability that it belongs to a female?

  c. A receipt for a glasscutter was dropped in the kitchen. What is the probability that the date of the purchase was on a day beginning with the letter T?

1. Put these in order from least to greatest.

$$\frac{2}{3} \qquad \frac{1}{2} \qquad \frac{3}{5} \qquad \frac{2}{9}$$

2. The phone at the Sure-Fire Detective Agency has rung 96 times in the past 12 hours. At this rate, how many times will the phone ring in the next three hours?

3. Compute: $\frac{5}{6} \div \frac{2}{3} =$

4. Estimate the area of this figure. Give your answer in square units.

5. Can this equation be used to solve the following problem?

$$x + (x + 2) + (x + 4) = 21$$

Detective Snoop kept a suspect under surveillance for several hours on Monday. On Tuesday and Wednesday, he increased his surveillance time by 2 hours each day. The total time he watched (Monday–Wednesday) was 21 hours. How long did he watch the suspect on Monday?

1. Compute:
$2,000.00 – $1,483.24 =

2. Tell what is meant by the **odds against** an outcome. Then decide if the statement in bold print is true.

> Inspector Smart has been given a tip that three suspects in a robbery are hiding in trash cans in the alley behind Market Street. Assume the tip is reliable. The inspector arrives to find 14 garbage cans in the alley. He looks in one.

> **The odds against finding a suspect in this can are $\frac{14}{3}$.**

3. What number has the opposite value from **20.04**?

4. Is the answer correct? If not, correct the error.

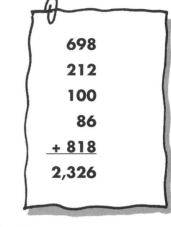

```
   698
   212
   100
    86
+ 818
 2,326
```

THE SUSPECTSs

Sam Shift

"Sneakers" LaRoux

Elaina E. Leusive

Clarisse B. Clever

5. Challenge Problem

Four suspects have been rounded up for possible involvement in the robbery and vandalizing of an ice cream shop. Use a trial and error strategy to figure out how old each suspect could be.

- The sum of their ages is 148.
- There are no odd numbers or odd digits.
- The product of Clarisse's and Elaina's ages is 2,400.
- Sneakers is eight years younger than Sam.
- The only digits found more than once in the ages are the digits 0 and 2.
- No age has the same digit twice.
- The ages are all < 62.

Name

1. There are 17 countries in the world with names beginning with the letter B. Jon chooses one at random. What is the probability that it will NOT be Belize, Botswana, or Burkina Faso?

2. Simplify the expression.

$$8b^2 - 7b + 4b^2 - b^2$$

Express yourself.

3. Canada has the longest coastline of any country. It is 202,080 km. China has 22,147 km of borders—more than any other country. What is the difference between the two lengths?

4. Angle A and Angle B are **supplementary angles**. Angle B measures 99°. What is the measure of Angle A?

5. The table shows the top five countries visited by tourists from outside the country. What was the average number of visitors to one of these countries in the year 2002?

THE NEW EXPLORER MAGAZINE

International Tourist Destinations

Country	Visitors
1. France	77,000,000
2. Spain	51,700,000
3. U.S.	41,900,000
4. Italy	39,800,000
5. China	36,800,000

Name

1. Compute:

$$\sqrt{121} - \sqrt{81} =$$

2. Each year, thousands of visitors travel to Stonehenge, England, to see the mysterious stone ruins. What is the surface area of this block of a stone ruin?

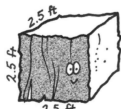

2.5 ft
2.5 ft
2.5 ft

3. Solve the equation:

$$150y = 30$$

4. Round to the nearest whole number:

$$46\frac{7}{11}$$

5. Kenyata flew from Spain to see the Great Barrier Reef off the east coast of Australia. This part of Australia is ten time zones east (earlier) of Spain's time zone. The flight took 11 hours and 42 minutes. Kenyata left Spain at 6:15 am on Monday. When did he arrive at his Australia destination (day and time)?

1. Change the different elements to a common element to solve the problem.

Students in a high school graduating class chose from four different trips. Sixteen percent of the 450 students went to Mali to see Timbuktu. Four- hundredths of the group went to see Roman ruins. One-third of the students chose to stand on the equator in Ecuador. The rest went to New Zealand. How many went to each destination?

2. Compute: **21 + -63 =**

3. Fill in the missing sign: **<, >,** or **=**

-52 ☐ **-36**

4. Name two real-life objects that are **prisms**.

5. What is the difference between the areas of the smallest country and the 10th smallest country?

Areas of Ten Smallest Countries

Country	Area sq mi	Country	Area sq mi
Vatican City	0.2	Liechtenstein	62
Monaco	0.7	Marshall Islands	70
Mauru	8	Maldives	115
Tuvalu	10	Malta	124
San Marino	23	Grenada	130

When it's 5:00 p.m., Tuesday, in the Vatican City, . . .

it's 5:00 a.m., Wednesday, in Tuvalu. It's a big world, full of small countries.

1. Compute:

$$\frac{1}{8} \times \frac{1}{5} =$$

2. Tyrone claims that he has hiked four kilometers a day in the Himalayan Mountain area. Is this a reasonable measurement?

3. Circle fractions equivalent to $\frac{2}{3}$.

$$\frac{6}{9} \qquad \frac{4}{9} \qquad \frac{18}{27} \qquad \frac{22}{33} \qquad \frac{8}{10}$$

4. Is this solution correct?

-20d = 36,000

d = 18,000

5. Solve the problem. Tell what operations were needed and the order in which you used them.

The country of Fiji is a collection of 332 islands. Palau is a country of 200 islands. The Bahamas has 700 islands. The country of Indonesia has 16.876 more islands than the sum of all the islands of Fiji, Palau, and the Bahamas. How many islands make up the country of Indonesia?

WOW!

Travel Brochure

1. Which equation has a correct solution?

equation	solution
a. $a^2 + 40 = 121$	$(a = 8)$
b. $\frac{896}{2x} = 224$	$(x = 2)$
c. $-15b = 990$	$(b = 66)$
d. $2000 = 50y$	$(y = 1000)$

2. What property is shown?

$$15(2 + 12) = (15 \times 2) + (15 \times 12)$$

3. Earth's total land mass (all the countries and territories combined) is approximately 57,500,000 square miles. Write this number in **scientific notation**.

4. What number is **205.5 less than 405**?

5. Challenge Problem

Find the percentages to answer the questions.

Tip:
When finding the percentage of a group of people, always round up to the nearest whole person.
(That makes sense, doesn't it?)

a. Uganda population – 26,404,540
About 50 percent of the population is under 15 years of age. How many are under 15?

b. Nepal area – 54,363 mi²
The Himalayan Mountain region covers 80 percent of Nepal's area. How much area is this?

c. Algeria area – 919,590 mi²
The Sahara Desert covers 85 percent of this country. How much area is this?

d. USA Population – 293,027,570
The adult literacy rate is 97 percent. How many adults in the USA cannot read? *(Round to nearest whole number.)*

e. Barbados Sunshine
The sun shines 70 percent of daytime hours (12-hour days) each year. How many hours of sunshine are there in a year in Barbados?

1. Solve the equation.

$$44 = -2w$$

2. There are eight black bulls, nine brown bulls, and one white bull in the pen. One bull is released.

   a. What is the probability that it will be a black bull?

   b. What is the probability that it will not be white?

3. Which operation should be done first?

$$2(3 - 5) + 12 =$$

4. How many edges are on a cylinder?

How many matadors will I beat today?

5. Use mental math to estimate the total amount of time of the bullfight activities.

Event	Time: min/sec
The presidente enters his box	1:14
Trumpet blows a fanfare	0:49
Alguaciles get the key to the toril	1:38
The paseo–parade of matadors	3:55
Bull enters	1:10
Banderilleros get bull to charge	2:40
Matador makes six passes	4:12
Picadors lance the bull	3:30
Banderilleros place banderillas in bull's neck	3:52
Matador performs passes with muleta	6:13
Matador kills the bull	0:47
Crowd cheers	2:15

1. Which fractions are in *lowest terms*?

$$\frac{6}{9} \quad \frac{3}{5} \quad \frac{5}{15}$$

$$\frac{12}{4} \quad \frac{7}{12} \quad \frac{4}{5}$$

2. How many *variables* are in this expression?

$$3b + 4c + 2b^2$$

3. Compute: $0.743 + 4.26 =$

4. One bullring (a perfect circle) has a 55-yard diameter. What is its area?

Let me calculate that.

5. Is this a problem that can be solved?

Bullfighting arenas have a wooden fence separating the ring from the spectator area. One arena has a ring that is 150 feet in diameter. The fence around it is five feet tall.

   a. What is the length of the fence that surrounds the ring?

   b. What is the area of the fence?

1. Which simplified equation is correct?

6n + 3n² – n + 6 = 48

a. $8n^2 + 6 = 48$

b. $5n + 3n^2 = 42$

c. $17n = 42$

d. $8n^2 = 42$

2. The Plaxa de Toras Monumental in Mexico City, the world's largest bullring, holds 55,000. Santo estimates that the bullring must have 366 sections of 150 seats. Are his calculations correct?

3. Compute: **–65 x –13 =**

4. Find the **mode** of this set of data.

Ages of the Matadors

36	18	22	19	24
19	23	27	26	33
20	32	23	30	35
23	34	28	31	23

Olé!

5. Draw two different trapezoids.

1. List the common factors of **60** and **45**.

Circle the **greatest common factor**.

2. Fill in the missing operation.

$$\frac{7}{3} \ \square \ \frac{5}{9} = 4\frac{1}{5}$$

3. What unit or units would be good choices for measuring the weight of the ring in the bull's nose?

4. Simplify the equation.

$$n = c^3 \cdot c^5$$

5. What generalization about Eduardo's career can you make from the data on the graph?

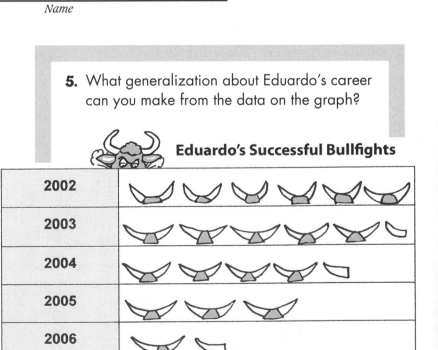

Eduardo's Successful Bullfights

2002	
2003	
2004	
2005	
2006	

= ten bullfights

1. Estimate the solution:

$$68 \times 212 =$$

2. Which conversions are correct?

    a. 40 cm = 4 m

    b. 20,000 mL = 20 L

    c. 30 ft = 10 yd

    d. 720 in = 60 ft

    e. 48 oz = 3 lb

    f. 5000 kg = 5 g

    g. 6 km = 660 m

3. Compute:

$$60,000 \div 30 =$$

4. Solve the equation. Show all your steps. Describe each step in words.

$$13p + 6 = 786$$

5. Challenge Problem

Show the statistics from the table in the form of a bar graph. Give the graph a title.

Bullring Seating Capacities	
Bullring	**Seats**
Marbella	9,500
San Isidro	25,000
Las Ventas	25,000
Plaza México	48,000
Plaza de Valencia	27,000
Campo Pequeño	10,000
Las Arenas de Barcelona	15,000
Maestranza	12,500

1. Compute: **17,963**
                  + 5,193

2. Solve the equation.

$$\frac{3}{4}n - \frac{1}{4}n = 40$$

3. These are the weights (in pounds) of trees Paul Bunyan hauled on his shoulder. What is the *median* in this set of data?

590	**660**	**790**
1110	**1000**	**720**	**660**

4. Draw a *flip* of this figure.

My tail isn't tall, but it's certainly long.

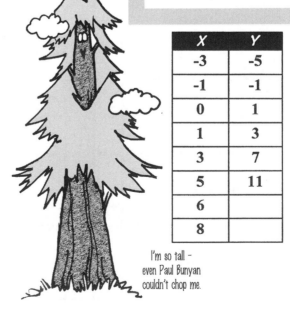

5. Convert all the measurements into pounds to compare the weights in these tall tales. Write the three items in order from lightest to heaviest.

- That fish I caught was so big that a picture of it weighed 12 kg.

- The mosquito was so big that it carried off a 272-ounce turtle.

- The spider was so big that she laid a 0.015-ton egg.

1. Most tall tales are about the weather. Many others are about a fish someone caught. During the two-week logging job, workers told 75 fish stories and 45 weather tales. What is the ratio of fish tales to weather tales?

2. Compute and round to nearest hundredth.

5.21 x 3.78 =

3. What formula would help Paul Bunyan find the volume of his cylindrical water container?

4. Paul Bunyan trained 2,000-lb ants to do logging work. This weight is closest to:

    a. 9,000 kg   c. 1,000 kg

    b. 440 kg   d. 900 kg

5. Write the function rule. Complete the function table.

X	Y
-3	-5
-1	-1
0	1
1	3
3	7
5	11
6	
8	

I'm so tall – even Paul Bunyan couldn't chop me.

1. Pecos Bill had four tasks to do one day, but he only had time to do two. The tasks were: riding a cyclone, lassoing a runaway train, rounding up 5,000 head of cattle, and draining the Rio Grande. How many combinations of two things are possible? Name them.

2. Compute:

$$3\overline{)-7,590}$$

3. True or false? A **tangent** is a line which touches a circle or other curve only at one point.

4. Simplify.

$$12 + s^3 - 20 = 56$$

5. Paul Bunyan and his lumberjacks eat so much that the cook needs to multiply this recipe by 20. Rewrite the recipe as it needs to read for Paul's crew.

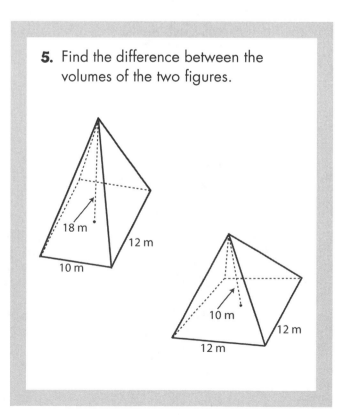

Lumberjack Stew

$2\frac{1}{4}$ lb....... beef cubes
$2\frac{1}{5}$ lb....... wild turkey meat
4 T...........crushed garlic
$3\frac{1}{2}$ lb....... sliced potatoes
$3\frac{1}{3}$ C........ carrot chunks
$2\frac{3}{4}$ C........ diced onions
3 T........... crushed oregano
5 qt......... beef broth

Combine all ingredients, and simmer over low fire for four hours.

1. Which operation should be done first?

$$7 + 5^2 - 6 =$$

2. Write an equation with integers to represent and solve this problem.

It was so cold last night that the stars froze! At midnight it was 14° below. By 4:00 a.m. the temperature had dropped 12°, and by 5:00 a.m. it had dropped another 25°. How cold was it then?

3. Compute: $\frac{3}{5} \div \frac{5}{6} =$

4. Jacob heard 140 campfire tales. 85 percent of them were tall tales. How many were not tall tales?

I've heard many tall tales around the campfire.

5. Find the difference between the volumes of the two figures.

18 m
12 m
10 m

10 m
12 m
12 m

1. Compute:

$$\frac{1}{3} \times 23.09 =$$

2. If a = 6, what is b?

$$a + 34 = -b$$

3. Compute:

$$\$1,548.09 \div 3 =$$

4. Which figures are **congruent** to **b**?

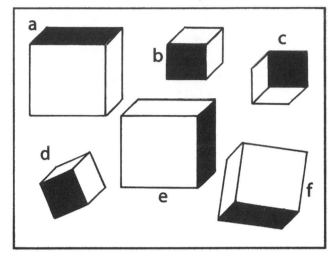

---

5. Challenge Problem

Write and use a proportion to solve each of the Paul Bunyan problems.

Stories about Paul Bunyan tell that he was much larger than the average lumberjack, that he had some interesting animal helpers, that he had some amazing abilities, and that he performed outrageous feats.

a. Paul straightened out two crooked rivers in five days. At this rate, how long would it take to straighten eight rivers?

b. It is said that, in one day, Paul could do the logging work that it would take 18 men to do. What could Paul accomplish in 12 days of work at this same rate?

c. Paul had a huge appetite. He could eat 22 flapjacks in three minutes. At this rate, how long would it take him to eat 88 flapjacks?

d. Paul's legs were so long that he could walk 28 miles with just 168 strides. At this rate, how far could he walk with 90 strides?

e. Paul could fell 84 trees every half-hour. How many trees could he fell in eight hours?

1. Brazil is number four on the list of nations with the most pet cats. The total of all the cats in the top ten nations is about 76,430,000. Brazil has about 16 percent of the total. What is Brazil's approximate cat population?

2. Compute:

2,346 ÷ 23 =

3. Three pets are racing: a cat, a ferret, and a rat. How many permutations are there for the order in which the three pets may finish the race?

4. Use words to write this expression.

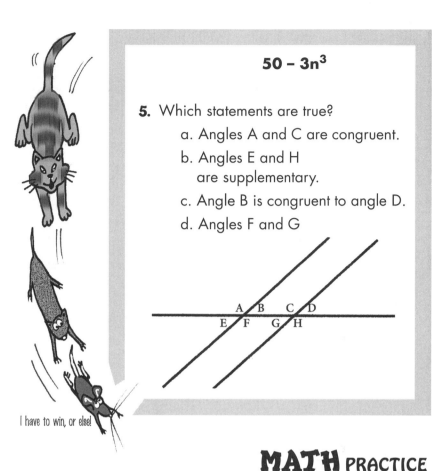

$50 - 3n^3$

5. Which statements are true?
   a. Angles A and C are congruent.
   b. Angles E and H are supplementary.
   c. Angle B is congruent to angle D.
   d. Angles F and G

I have to win, or else!

1. Raymond wants to buy a pet skunk that is on sale for $13.99. Raymond has 28 quarters, 117 nickels, and 7 pennies. Can he afford the skunk?

2. Compute:

$0.5 \overline{)2.5}$

I wonder how much a *quarter* of a skunk costs?

3. Simplify the equation.

$\frac{48}{3} - b^2 = 0$

4. Find the volume of this figure.

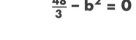
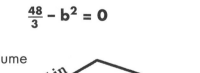

7 in

10 in

2 in

5. Use mental math to solve the problem.

An animal shelter has a large number of small pets they must give away quickly. There are 34 mice, 26 hamsters, and 19 cats. Eight people have offered to adopt the pets. Describe a way to distribute the pets nearly evenly to the eight homes. Each home should have some of each kind of pet.

1. Compute: **–82 + 37 – (–10) =**

    a. 95   c. –35

    b. 35   d. –140

2. Solve the equation.

$$\frac{6}{7} = \frac{x}{84}$$

3. A cage had six white and six brown mice. Luke reached in and grabbed one without looking. He got a white one. He reached in again to get a second mouse. What is the probability that he will get another white mouse?

4. Which figure has more faces: a cube or a hexagonal prism?

I'd make a great pencil pet.

5. Make the changes in the results of a pet survey at a local school.

    a. 35% of the pet owners had cats. Change this to a decimal.

    b. $\frac{8}{10}$ of the pet owners had dogs. Change this to a percent.

    c. $\frac{14}{100}$ of the pet owners had both a cat and a dog. Write this as a decimal.

    d. 21 of the pet owners had birds. There were 140 pet owners. Write the number of bird owners as a percent.

1. Solve the proportion.

$$\frac{65}{x} = \frac{117}{9}$$

2. Compute: $\frac{3}{5} + 1\frac{3}{6} =$

3. Louie's pet snake, Louise, gets exercise by crawling around a pentagon with sides that measure 9.5 m each. If Louise completes the route three times, how far does she crawl?

4. Fill in the missing symbol:

    <, >, or =

$$7 + \sqrt{144} \boxed{} 42$$

5. Follow these clues to find the age of Suzy, the oldest living pet pony.

- It is a two-digit even number.
- The sum of the digits is 9.
- The two digits are different numbers.
- All digits are < 7 and > 1.
- The product of the digits is 20.
- The first digit > than the second.

It might help to draw a pentagon.

1. Which example does not show the ***identity property***?

   a. $\frac{7}{10} \times 1 = \frac{7}{10}$

   b. $0 \times 4.509 = 0$

   c. $16.16 + 0 = 16.16$

   d. $80,000 \div 1 = 80,000$

2. Is this solution accurate?

   4,363 ÷ 7 = 623 R 4

3. Find **k** if **g** = –20.

   5k – 10 = g

4. Make a circle graph that shows the division of the $540 Sandy spends on her cat each year. She spends $30 on toys, $30 on grooming, $180 on litter, $240 on food, and $60 on vet bills.

5. Challenge Problem

Use the data on the graph to answer the question: Which kinds of pets had a general increase in popularity over the 16-year period?

What, no rats?

•－－• DOGS
•－－• CATS
•━━• HAMSTERS
•－•－• BIRDS
•∙∙∙∙• EXOTIC PETS

PET CHOICES, STUDENTS AT BLY MIDDLE SCHOOL
(1990-2006)

1990 1992 1994 1996 1998 2000 2002 2004 2006

1. Bob has a bag of 20 light bulbs. Four of them are burned out. He reaches in the bag and grabs a bulb. What is the probability that he will get a good bulb?

2. Simplify the equation.

   $$6(5 + x) = 16x$$

3. Charlie wants to show how the cost of electrical power differs in six countries. What is the best way to do this?

   ○ histogram   ○ tally sheet

   ○ bar graph   ○ pictograph

4. True or false?
   A rhombus is a four-sided figure with no right angles.

I get a charge out of math.

5. Scientist Dr. Sparks counted the flashes of lightning he saw around his home town for three months. He saw 25 in June, 51 in July, and 62 in August.

   a. What is the average number a month?

   b. What is the average number he saw in a day?

1. Lightning struck in Taylor's back yard at 3:30 p.m. It struck again at 2:57 a.m. the next morning. About how much time elapsed between the two strikes?

2. Compute:

   $$4.042 \times 1{,}000 =$$

3. Use words to write this expression.

   $$3n^3 > 100$$

4. Round to the nearest hundredth:

   20.0873

5. The St. Pierre family uses this container to catch rain during the big thunderstorms they get in the summer. Find the volume of this container.

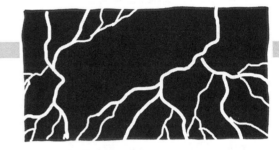

This is a strange birdfeeder.

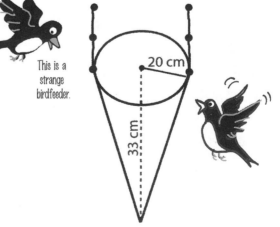

20 cm

33 cm

1. Compute:

$$-84\overline{)-32{,}424}$$

2. What formula will solve the problem?

A storm is traveling at two miles per hour (r). Right now, at 8:00 p.m., the storm is seven miles away (d). When will it arrive (t)?

3. Name this space figure:

4. A store is giving away some electronic games. There are 200 of them, all in the original packages. Fifteen of the games are defective and do not work. What are the odds against getting one that works?

5. Three friends are hurrying home in a rainstorm. Each friend has a different color umbrella. Follow the clues to find out who had which umbrella and who got home first.

- Roz does not have the green umbrella.

- Zack did not get home first.

- Jessie got home before Zack.

- The person with the black umbrella got home first.

- The person with the red umbrella got home after Zack.

1. Compute:

$$1\tfrac{1}{2} \times 2\tfrac{2}{3} =$$

2. What is the least common multiple of **3** and **27**?

3. Simplify the expression.

$$-30 + d - 12 + 6d$$

4. In early January of 2010, Mr. Grafton learned that his electric bill was expected to increase 81 percent by the end of June, 2014. What will be the average monthly increase (in percent)?

I light up your life.

5. Solve the problem by translating it into an equation.

In its first month of operation, America's first power station produced enough power to light a certain number of light bulbs. Within 14 months, the plant was producing 15 times that much power. The sum of the bulbs lit in the 1st month and in the 14th month is 6,400 bulbs. How many bulbs could be lit with the power produced in this first month?

Name

1. Fill in the missing operation.

$$0.06 \;\boxed{}\; 0.7 = 0.042$$

2. Compute: $-88 \div \sqrt{64} =$

3. What is the probability that one spin of this spinner will result in black thunder?

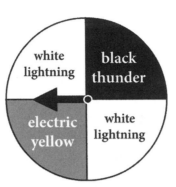

4. Follow the function rule to replace the missing numbers.

x = y − 3	
x	**y**
-3	
	1
-1	
	0
1	4
	5
3	

5. Challenge Problem

A high school swim team got ready to sell holiday lights as a fundraiser. They bought a supply of 8,000 strands of miniature lights. The coach took home a few strings and found that some are defective. So the team decided to do random sampling to find out how many of the strings of lights might not be in perfect condition.

They tested a group of 100 strings, and found that 8 out of the 100 would not light up. They found another 10 in the sample that had at least one light that would not work, though the rest of the lights were fine.

a. Predict the number of strands (out of the total 8,000) that will not light up at all.

b. Predict the number of strands (out of the total 8,000) that will have lights that don't work, even though most of the string will light up.

c. Predict the number of strands (out of the total 8,000) that will be defective in some way.

I lost my sparkle.

1. A cheetah (the fastest animal) can run about 25 km in 15 minutes. The slowest animal, a snail, runs about 0.0125 km in the same amount of time. What are the rates per hour of these animals?

2. Compute: **440 x 108 =**

3. Solve the equation: $5\frac{1}{2}y = 420$

4. Which figures are similar to the first one?

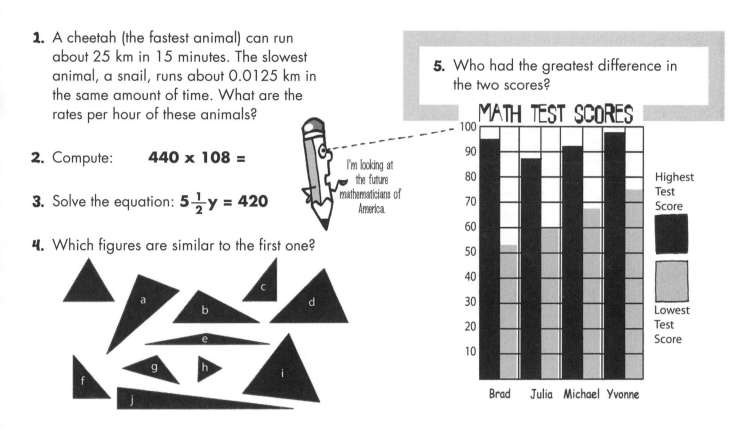

I'm looking at the future mathematicians of America.

5. Who had the greatest difference in the two scores?

MATH TEST SCORES

Highest Test Score

Lowest Test Score

Brad   Julia   Michael   Yvonne

1. Is the computation correct?

12.2 + 9.07 – 3.004 = 18.266

2. The Nile River is the longest river in the world at 4,145 mi. The Roe River is the shortest river. The difference is 4,144 mi, 5060 ft. How long is the Roe?

3. Put these in order from **greatest** to **least**.

30,303,333   30,330,030   30,330,003

4. What is the perimeter of this figure?

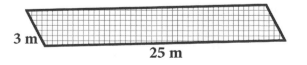

3 m

25 m

5. Use estimation to solve the problem.

A koala bear sleeps 22 hours a day. A zebra sleeps three hours a day. What is the difference in the amount of sleep these two animals will get in a year?

It sounds as if koalas make pretty good pets.

Name

1. Simplify the expression.

$$15k^8 \div 3k^2$$

2. A Cuban arrow-poison frog is only 1.2 cm long. An Arctic giant jellyfish can grow to about 29,166 times the frog's length. How long is this? *(Round to the nearest ten.)*

3. Compute: **4,321 x –20 =**

4. Will has a bag of 1,000 black and white jellybeans. Of the first 50 beans he takes out of the bag, 38 are black. If the number of black beans in the bag is proportional to the first 50, how many white beans would be in the bag of 1,000?

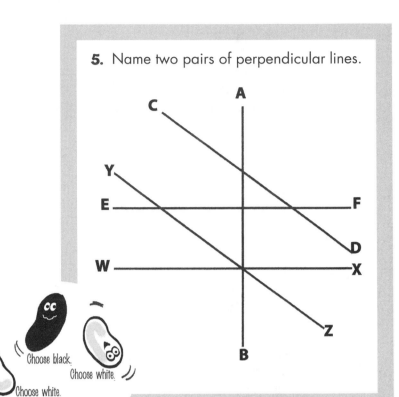

5. Name two pairs of perpendicular lines.

Name

1. What is the value of the 3?

42,397,655

2. Compute: $\frac{1}{2} \times \frac{9}{6} =$

3. Solve the equation.

$$10y + 7 = 4y + 43$$

4. Find the volume of this figure.

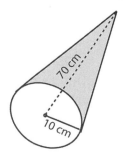

70 cm

10 cm

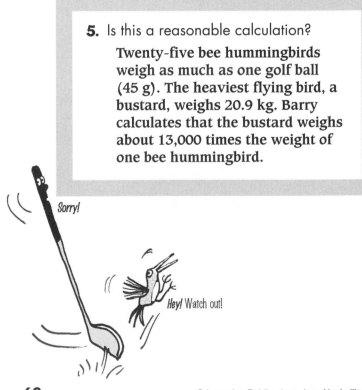

5. Is this a reasonable calculation?

Twenty-five bee hummingbirds weigh as much as one golf ball (45 g). The heaviest flying bird, a bustard, weighs 20.9 kg. Barry calculates that the bustard weighs about 13,000 times the weight of one bee hummingbird.

Sorry!

Hey! Watch out!

1. Is this an accurate solution to the equation?

$$6(b - 5) + b^2 = 82$$
$$b = 8$$

2. Show $\frac{4}{5}$ as a decimal and a percent.

3. What property is shown here?

$$(60 + 3,400) + 9,000 = 60 + (3,400 + 9,000)$$

4. Write this problem using the inverse operation.

$$32,675 - 28,423 = 4,252$$

5. Challenge Problem

On Saturday, Theresa and Ted did something quite opposite of their usual behavior. Instead of buying new stuff for themselves, they decided to give away things—including some of their things that they still used and liked. They arrived back home at 2:08 p.m. Use the strategy of working backwards to find out what time they started their day's adventure.

Activity	Time Taken
Found stuff in closets	25 min
Found stuff in drawers	12 min
Found stuff in garage	14 min
Found stuff in basement	15 min
Loaded the car	11 min
Picked up more stuff from friends	1 hr, 10 min
Drove to, unloaded at child care center	1 hr, 6 min
Drove to, unloaded at Goodwill	45 min
Drove to, unloaded at church	53 min
Drove home	27 min

Quick! Calculate the time before they give the clock away!

1. Compute: 100,000
                  − 89,898

2. Give a definition of **frequency** of an item in a set of data.

3. Write an equation that will solve this problem.

> Julianna takes people on tours of ancient Egyptian sites five days a week. On Mondays, Wednesdays, and Fridays, the tours are three hours long. Her total tour time each week is 20 hours. How long are the Tuesday and Thursday tours? (They are the same length.)

4. Give two characteristics of a **pyramid**.

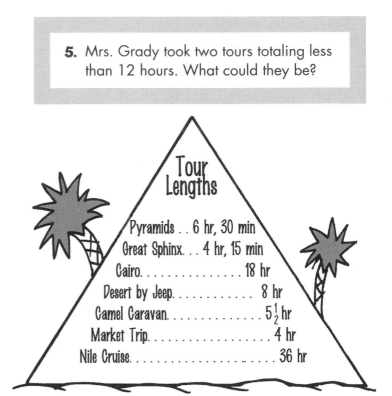

5. Mrs. Grady took two tours totaling less than 12 hours. What could they be?

Tour Lengths

Pyramids . . 6 hr, 30 min
Great Sphinx. . 4 hr, 15 min
Cairo. . . . . 18 hr
Desert by Jeep. . . . . 8 hr
Camel Caravan. . . . . $5\frac{1}{2}$ hr
Market Trip. . . . . 4 hr
Nile Cruise. . . . . 36 hr

1. Kate's plane ticket to Egypt cost $1,148.00. Taxes and surcharges of 23 percent were added to that amount. What was the total cost?

2. Find **m** if **g** = 13.

$$7g - 4g = m + 20$$

3. The Great Pyramid was built with two million limestone blocks. One hundred of these weighed 230 metric tons. Write a proportion to find the weight of 15 of the blocks.

4. Round to the nearest thousand.

63,468,895

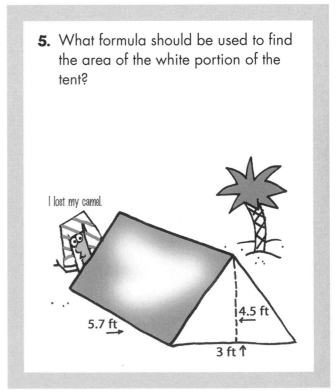

5. What formula should be used to find the area of the white portion of the tent?

I lost my camel.

5.7 ft

4.5 ft

3 ft ↑

1. Compute:

$$-87 - 50 - (-3) =$$

2. What space figure has seven faces?

3. Mark won a trip to Egypt. He was assigned a month of the year at random for his travels. What is the probability that he was assigned a month that does not have 31 days?

4. Simplify the expression:

$$\frac{88b}{4}$$

Four thousand years of dust storms, and I still look pretty sharp.

5. The base of the Great Pyramid covers an area of 13 acres. An acre is 4,840 square yards. If the base of the pyramid is a square, what is the length of each side of the base?

  a. about 1,000 yards

  b. about 22 yards

  c. about 250 yards

  d. about 1,400 yards

1. The height of the Great Sphinx in Egypt (in meters) can be found by solving this problem:

$$6 \times \sqrt{121} =$$

I hope this isn't another pyramid.

2. Compute: $\frac{3}{3} + \frac{4}{3} =$

3. Write this number in standard notation.

thirty-five million, one hundred four thousand, two hundred two

4. An archaeologist worked in Egypt, digging and exploring in ruins. She was there from June 1, 2003 through March 15, 2005. How many days was this?

5. Plot these points. Connect them with a line. Name the figure.

(–3, 3); (–2, –2); (2, –2); (3, 3)

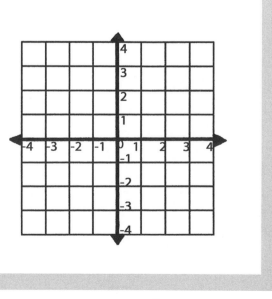

1. Compute: **400 x 700,000 =**

2. The largest pyramid in Egypt is the Great Pyramid. This structure is 140 meters tall. This measurement is about

    a. 47 feet   c. 5600 feet

    b. 4500 feet   d. 450 feet

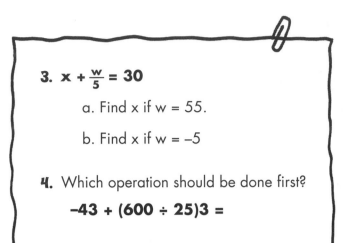

3. $x + \frac{w}{5} = 30$

    a. Find x if w = 55.

    b. Find x if w = –5

4. Which operation should be done first?

$$-43 + (600 \div 25)3 =$$

5. Challenge Problem

Describe the information that is needed to solve each problem.

    a. The Sahara Desert could cover the entire continental United States. A camel moves at a speed of about three miles an hour. How long would it take a camel to cross the Sahara Desert?

    b. King Tutankhamen, one of the most famous of the Egyptian pharaohs, was born in 1347 BC. How old was he when he died?

    c. The ancient Egyptians developed an elaborate process for preparing mummies. How long ago was this process developed?

    d. The Nile River is the longest river in the world. It is 151 miles longer than the world's second longest river, the Amazon. How long is the Amazon?

Mummy-making is an elaborate process, all right.

    e. Some sand dunes in Africa's Sahara Desert are as tall as 1,526 feet. How much taller is this than the height of the Eiffel Tower?

1. By the mid 1950s, the term *flying saucer* was familiar to 94 percent of Americans. If a town had a population of 13,650, how many of its people would have been familiar with the term?

2. Compute:

$$23 \overline{)4,897}$$

I'm famous wherever I go.

3. What is the **coefficient** of the variable **b**?

$$9a + 16b - 6a = 86$$

4. Draw a figure similar to this one.

5. Someone spins this spinner once. Find the probabilities described below.

a. P 5 =

b. P not 9 =

c. P not 2 and not 4 =

1. The Bermuda Triangle has its endpoints in Miami, Florida, San Juan, Puerto, Rico, and the Bahamas. The legs of the triangle measure 965 mi, 1,038 mi, and 1,042 mi. What is the perimeter?

2. Which numbers are divisible by **7**?

147   307   87   175   717

3. Simplify the equation.

$$5n + 2n + 20 = 86 - 4n$$

4. Compute; round the answer to the nearest tenth:

$$\begin{array}{r} 4.03 \\ \times\ 2.15 \\ \hline \end{array}$$

5. Tell what operations you would use to solve this problem, and in what order you would use them.

Bradley boldly took trips across the Bermuda Triangle. Every month from January through August, he took ten trips across the area. During the other months, he took 14 trips. How many trips did he take all together in three years?

Look, I drew the Bermuda Triangle.

1. Compute:

$$7\overline{)-354}$$

2. Detective Ivan Surch keeps track of reports of strange disappearances. He had 25 reports a week for five weeks. There were 17 reports in week six, 39 in week seven, and 28 in week eight. What is the average number of reports per week?

3. Which values could replace **b** in the statement **4b + 2 > –3**?

3   4   –2   –4   –1   0

4. Draw a scalene triangle.

5. Captain Ed kept a count of people who reported seeing ghost ships. What is the total number of reports?

I love ghostly statistics.

Reports of Ghost Ship Sightings

Flying Dutchman	卌 卌 卌 卌 II
crew from SS Waterloo	卌 卌 卌 III
SS Iron Mountain	卌 II
The Griffin	卌 卌 卌
The Emperor	卌 卌 II

1. Fill in the missing symbol: **<. >**, or **=**

$$\frac{8}{11} \; \boxed{} \; \frac{4}{5}$$

2. Is this pair of numbers **(–10, –2)** as (x, y) a solution for the equation?

$$\frac{3x}{5} + 2y = y + 4$$

3. The temperature of the waters in the Bermuda Triangle rose to 73°F. This is about

○ **181°C**   ○ **55°C**

○ **28°C**   ○ **113°C**

4. Compute: $\frac{5}{6} \times \frac{5}{11}$

Draw on your mental resources and solve the problem.

5. A recent poll found that a surprising percentage of people in the United States believe their government has withheld information about UFOs. Follow the clues to find the percentage.

- two odd digits (different)
- second digit < the first
- sum of digits > 6
- difference between digits > 4, < 7
- 3 is not one of the digits

1. Estimate the number of UFO sightings.

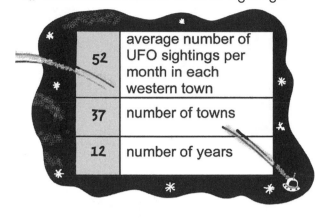

52	average number of UFO sightings per month in each western town
37	number of towns
12	number of years

2. Compute: $2{,}400^5 \div 2{,}400^3 =$

3. Solve the equation.

$$\tfrac{2}{3}n + 4 = 10$$

4. a. Which angles are supplementary to B?

   b. Which angle is congruent to D?

   c. Which angles are supplementary to C?

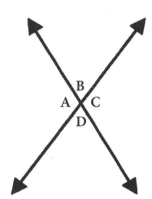

5. Challenge Problem

a. Count the triangles in the figure.

b. Count the parallelograms in the figure.

c. Count the trapezoids in the figure.

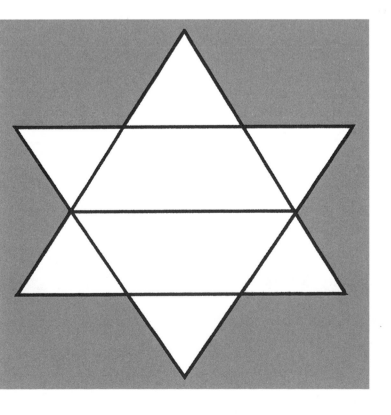

1. Compute: **5,555 x 22 =**

2. Use mental math to solve the problem.

Submarines have a cylindrical shape with slightly pointed ends that make them look somewhat like bullets. Estimate the volume of a sub with a six-meter diameter and a length of 98 m.

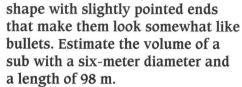

I always draw the line.

3. Simplify the equation.

5(p − 4) − 12 = 2p + 4

4. A countess owns a catamaran, a yacht, a jet ski, and a speedboat. She takes two of them out on the sea today. How many different combinations are possible? Name them.

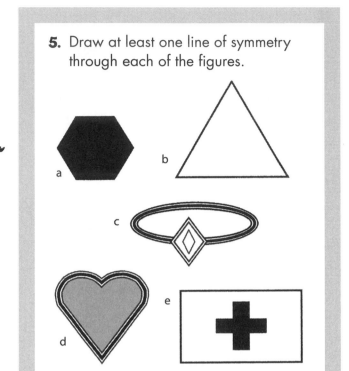

5. Draw at least one line of symmetry through each of the figures.

a

b

c

d

e

1. Write a proportion to solve the problem.

Georgia takes her sailboat out 15 times in the first three months of the year. At this rate, how many months will it take for her to go sailing 45 times?

2. Solve to find **h** if **k** = −6.

$$\frac{10k}{15} - h = 10$$

3. The fastest sailing vessel can sail about $53\frac{1}{2}$ miles per hour. Another ship sails at three-quarters of its speed. How fast does the second ship travel?

4. Compute: **39 ÷ 3.25 =**

You'll sail right through these problems.

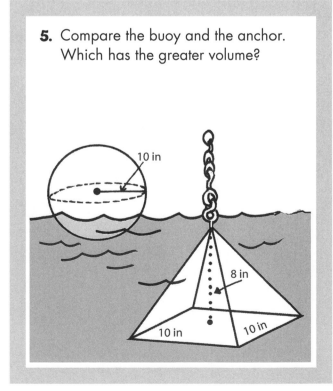

5. Compare the buoy and the anchor. Which has the greater volume?

10 in

8 in

10 in   10 in

1. Compute: **–200 – (–53) + 124 – 66 =**
  ○ **205**   ○ **–147**   ○ **58**
  ○ **–89**   ○ **89**   ○ **380**

2. Use words to write this expression.
$$10 - n^3 + n^2$$

3. What is the range of these yacht sizes?
  ○ **37 ft**   ○ **12 ft**   ○ **46 ft**   ○ **88 ft**
  ○ **112 ft**   ○ **92 ft**   ○ **130 ft**   ○ **125 ft**

I've come to see the regatta.

5. Solve the problem. Tell how you reached your solution.

A large ferry has a space for cars that is 510 feet long and 70 feet wide. Assume that each vehicle needs an area 8 feet long and 7 feet wide. How many vehicles can the boat carry at one time?

4. Name the figure that is the shape of each sail.

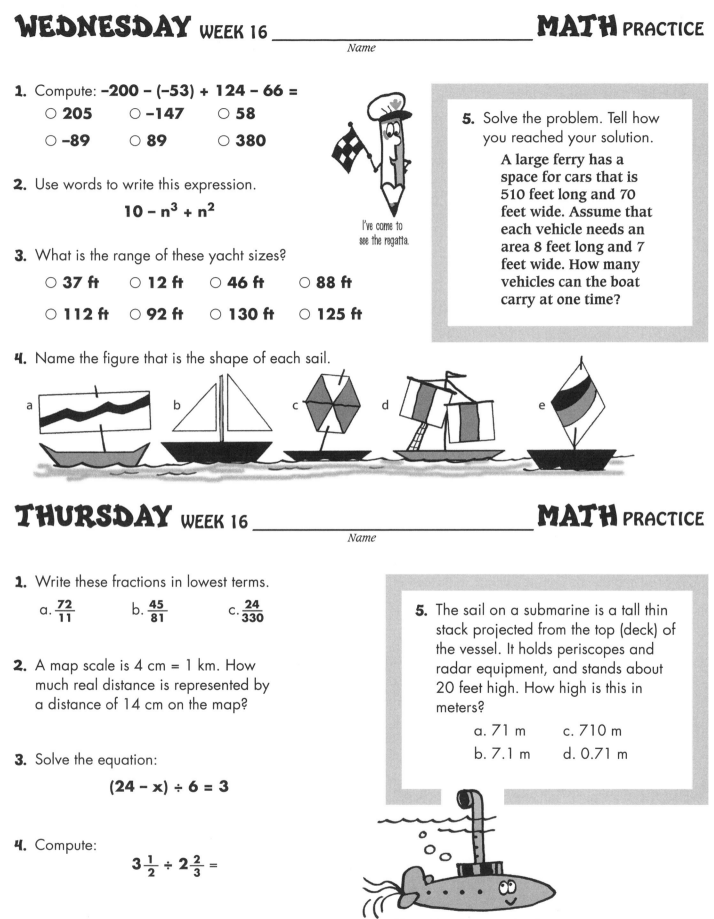

a   b   c   d   e

1. Write these fractions in lowest terms.
  a. $\frac{72}{11}$ b. $\frac{45}{81}$ c. $\frac{24}{330}$

2. A map scale is 4 cm = 1 km. How much real distance is represented by a distance of 14 cm on the map?

3. Solve the equation:
$$(24 - x) \div 6 = 3$$

4. Compute:
$$3\frac{1}{2} \div 2\frac{2}{3} =$$

5. The sail on a submarine is a tall thin stack projected from the top (deck) of the vessel. It holds periscopes and radar equipment, and stands about 20 feet high. How high is this in meters?
  a. 71 m   c. 710 m
  b. 7.1 m   d. 0.71 m

It's a good thing submarines are submersible.

1. Is the following solution correct?

$$3\frac{1}{2} \times \frac{5}{14} = 1\frac{1}{4}$$

2. Write a definition of **_opposite numbers_**.

3. Compute: **(15 x 10) ÷ 2.5 =**

4. There are five envelopes. Three each hold $100, the other two each hold $50. Rob draws one envelope. At the same time, he tosses a coin. List all the possible outcomes of these two events.

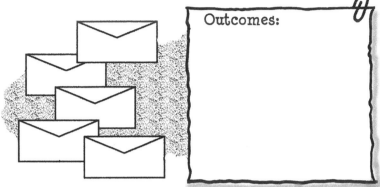

Outcomes:

5. Challenge Problem

The grid represents the location of shipwrecks.

a. Which kind of vessel is at (–4, –1)?

b. Write the coordinates for all the submarines.

c. Which kind of vessel is at (–4, 3)?

d. Which kind of vessel is at (4, –2)?

e. Draw a submarine at (–2, 0) and (1, –4).

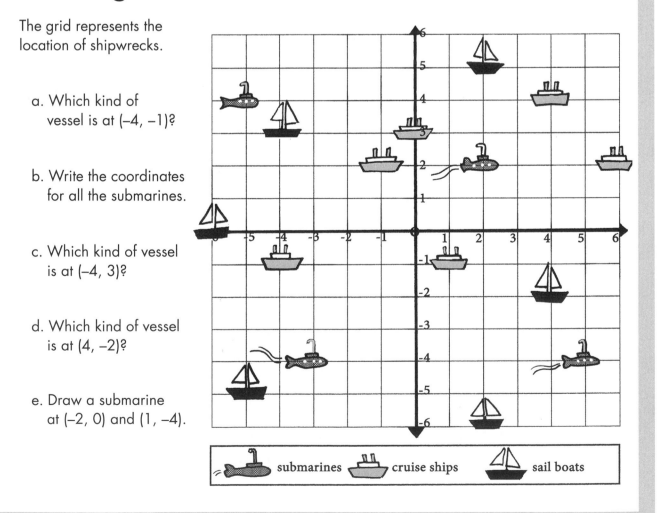

submarines   cruise ships   sail boats

1. How many congruent angles are found in an *isosceles triangle*?

2. Solve the equation.

$$-6 - 6x - (-4x) + 12 = 116$$

3. Compute: $400,000 \div 200 =$

4. A fishbowl contains three black fish, four silver fish, and five goldfish. Louie dips a net in and, without looking, catches a goldfish. He dips a second time. What is the probability that the second catch will also be a goldfish?

5. Solve the problem. Tell how you solved it.

A sailfish is the fastest fish in the sea. Its top speed is 68 mph. Assuming the sailfish can maintain this speed for a while, how far can it swim in 18 minutes?

1. Use the inverse operation to verify the accuracy of the computation.

$$72.3 - 63.04 = 9.26$$

2. Solve the equation.

$$70 - 5b = 14 + b$$

3. What is the value of the underlined place?

6,839.08<u>1</u>9

4. Find the volume of the fish bowl.

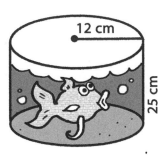

5. Tell what information is missing that would make this a problem that can be solved.

A blue tuna fish can swim 46 miles per hour. How much faster is this than the fastest human swimmer?

1. Compute: $-8.4\overline{\smash{\big)}77.28}$

2. Louisa has a huge aquarium containing six different kinds of fish. What kind of a graph would be best for showing the proportion of each kind of fish in her aquarium?

   ○ **bar graph**   ○ **line graph**

   ○ **double bar graph**   ○ **circle graph**

   ○ **double line graph**   ○ **pictograph**

3. Write this expression in words.

$$n(-3 + y)$$

4. A tiger shark covers a distance of 6.6 miles in 12 minutes. What is the shark's rate in miles per hour?

5. Name the transformation shown here.

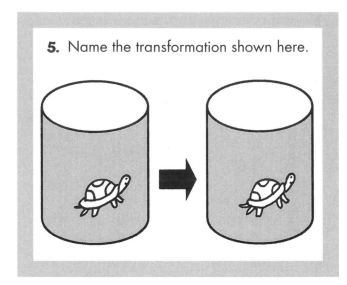

---

1. Which operation should be done first?

$$3x \div (4 + 8) + 2 = 7$$

2. Which fractions are equivalent to $\frac{2}{5}$?

   ○ $\frac{9}{20}$ ○ $\frac{12}{15}$ ○ $\frac{9}{10}$

   ○ $\frac{22}{55}$ ○ $\frac{15}{25}$ ○ $\frac{5}{10}$

I hate my job!

3. Compute: $12\frac{1}{10} - 7\frac{3}{10} =$

4. An ocean temperature was measured to be 20°C. What is this temperature in Fahrenheit?

35° 30° 25° 20° 15° 10° 5° 0

Centigrade

5. What is the best choice for the solution to the problem?

In Iceland, 15,000 people go fishing every day! Commercial fishing is a strong part of the economy of this island nation with a population of about 282,000. Approximately what percent of the population goes fishing each day?

   ○ **15%**

   ○ **5%**

   ○ **30%**

   ○ **19%**

1. Which example shows the **commutative property**?

  a. (80 + 13)5 = 80 x 5 + 13 x 5

  b. −395 + 395 = 0

  c. 0.3 + 1.6 = 1.6 + 0.3

  d. (4x + 9) + 5x = 4x + (9 + 5x)

2. Fill in the missing operation.

$$\sqrt{289} \ \boxed{} \ \frac{5}{8} = 16\frac{3}{8}$$

3. Simplify the expression. **n(8n − 6)**

4. Use words to write this expression.

$$10^2 − (p + 5)$$

5. Challenge Problem

Write T (true) or F (false) for each statement.
  a. The numbers in the union of **glad fish** and **sad fish** are all odd numbers.
  b. The numbers in the intersection of the **glad fish** and the **mad fish** total 101.
  c. The numbers in the intersection of all three figures are all even numbers.
  d. There are five numbers in the intersection of the **sad fish** and the **mad fish**.
  e. The total of numbers in the **sad fish** > the total of numbers in the **mad fish**.
  e. The numbers in the intersection of the **glad fish** and the **sad fish** total 125.

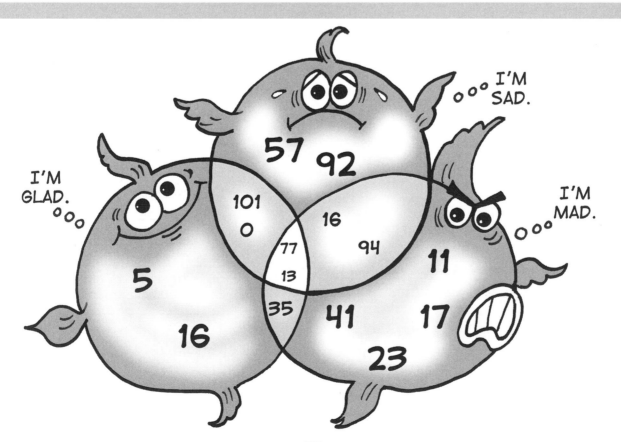

1. Name this figure.

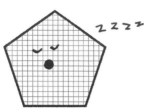

2. Simplify the equation.

30q – 65 = q + 80

3. Compute: **345,123**
– 10,824

4. The animated film *Finding Nemo* earned $70,251,710 in its first weekend at the box office. It played in 3,374 theaters that weekend. What was the average amount earned in each theater?

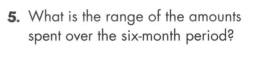

Does that include popcorn and a soda?

5. What is the range of the amounts spent over the six-month period?

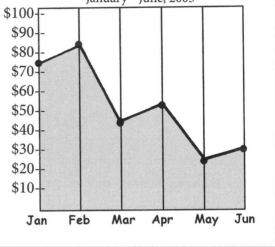

McMann Family Movie Expenditures
January - June, 2005

1. Compute:

$$6.003\overline{)1800.9}$$

2. Joe's favorite movie is three hours and 13 minutes long. He converted the measurement to 193 seconds. Is this reasonable?

3. Is this a correct graph of the statement **x < 3**?

4. Of the ten highest-earning movies in the U.S., one was an animated film. What is the ratio of non-animated films to animated films in the top ten?

5. The Sanchez family wants to see a movie on Tuesday at 3:00 p.m. They need four adult tickets (reg. price $8) and six child tickets (reg $3.50). Can they do this for under $40?

CINEMA BOX OFFICE

Early Bird Special
All Tickets **25%** off
regular prices
noon - **5:00 p.m.** Mon-Thurs.

TICKET WINDOW

1. A box holds movie tickets. Three are for an action movie, two are for a comedy, and one is for an animated film. Lucy draws two tickets. What is the probability that she will get one action movie ticket and one comedy ticket?

2. Compute: **4,500 − (−4,500) =**

3. Eight U.S. currency bills total $77. What could these be?

4. Which angle is supplementary to Angle EBC?

5. Choose the equation that can be used to solve the problem.

> **Universal City, Los Angeles, California, is the largest film studio complex in the world. The site is called the Back Lot. It has a total of 595 buildings and soundstages. The number of buildings is 17 more than 14 times the number of soundstages. How many soundstages are there on the Back Lot?**

a. $595 = x(17 + 14)$

b. $595 − 17x = 14$

c. $(17 + 14s) + s = 595$

d. $17(14 + x) = 595$

1. Write an equation with integers to find the balance of money in Jonathan's account.

> **Jonathan had $45 in his bank account. He withdrew $31 on Saturday to buy food for his Academy Awards party. On Monday, he wrote a $39 check to the movie theater. On Tuesday, he wrote another check for $17.**

2. Compute: $\frac{7}{9} \times \frac{3}{5} =$

3. Circle the units that can measure capacity.

gram	milliliter
pint	square kilometer
quart	kilogram
liter	acre

Just imagine all the Oscar Night parties in my honor.

4. Fill in the missing sign: **<, >,** or **=**

22.0022 ☐ **22.00202**

5. Give the function rule. Finish writing the ordered pairs.

x	y	(x, y)
-3	6	(-3, 6)
-2	4	( )
-1	2	( )
0	0	( )
1	-2	( )
2	-4	( )
3	-6	( )

Name

1. These are the amounts of money Max and Maxie spent on popcorn and treats at the movies in the past six visits to the theater. What was the average amount they spent each time?

$ 6.40	Apr 3
9.00	Apr 7
3.50	Apr 14
9.00	Apr 22
3.50	Apr 27
7.00	Apr 30

2. Write the value of each number.

a. 3.2×10^7

b. 5.55×10^4

c. 6.09×10^5

3. Solve the equation. $15 + 6y^2 = 231$

4. Which operation should be done first?

$$\$523.00 - \$23.60 - 3(\$0.20 + \$13.00) =$$

Going to the movies is so much fun!

5. Challenge Problem

a. What information is needed to find the number of theaters in India?

b. How much is spent on movies per person in Luxembourg?

c. What is the difference between the number of movie theaters in China and Canada?

d. What is the sum of the per person movie theater expenditure in Iceland and Ireland?

Most Movie Theaters

	Country	Movie Screens
1	China	65,500
2	USA	35,289
3	India	
4	France	5.280
5	Germany	4,868
6	Spain	4,093
7	Italy	3,495
8	UK	3,402
9	Mexico	2,755
10	Canada	2,753
	Total	

Money Spent on Movies

	Country	$ per person at Theaters
1	USA	$ 6.09
2	Iceland	$ 5.71
3	Australia	$ 4.95
4	Singapore	$ 4.91
5	N Zealand	$ 4.73
6	Ireland	$ 4.68
7	Canada	$ 4.22
8	Spain	$ 3.58
9	Luxembourg	
10	France	$ 3.14
	Total	$45.31

1. How many different **permutations** are possible for 4 people waiting in line to get on an airplane?

2. Compute:

$$32\overline{)27,520}$$

3. At any given hour, there are 61,000 people in the air (in airplanes) over the United States. How many people are up in planes over a 24-hour period?

4. Solve the equation.

$$\frac{x}{12} + \frac{6}{8} = 1$$

5. The wind is blowing, and kites are flying high in the air. Name the shape of each kite.

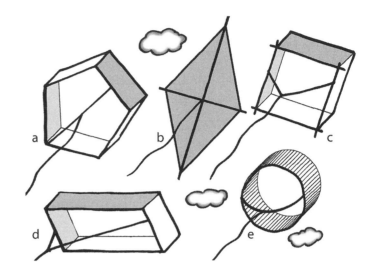

1. What unit of measure is appropriate to measure:

    a. the length of an airport runway?

    b. the capacity of a hot-air balloon?

    c. the surface area on a kite?

    d. the length of a flight from Miami to Chicago?

2. Solve the equation.

$$-13g = 91.52$$

3. The total cost of seven airplane tickets is $2,555.70. What is the average cost of each one?

4. Round to the nearest hundredth:

365.097

5. What is the difference between the number of seats in the main cabin and the number in the first-class cabin?

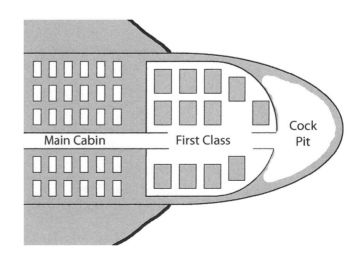

1. Compute: **−3,800 ÷ (−50) =**

2. Identify the figures that make up this plane.

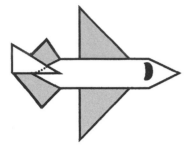

3. Find **b** if **a = −5.**

$$-40a + 7b = 95$$

4. Is 6,000 a good estimate for the solution to this problem?

8(6,888 − 1,111) + 12,895 =

5. Use the data to draw a conclusion about the changes in flight hours (for these flight attendants) from January to February.

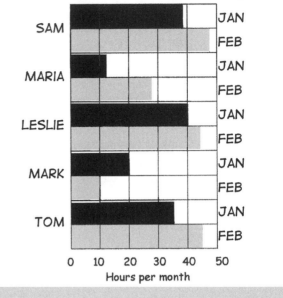

1. Change to a fraction: **7.088**

2. Draw the graph of this number sentence.

x = < 10

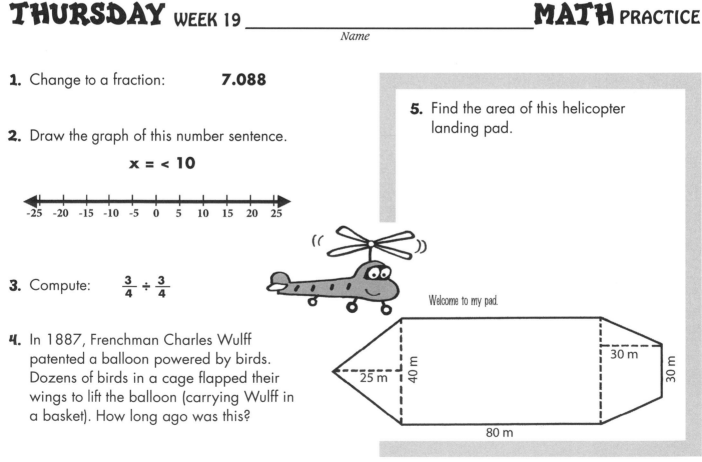

3. Compute: $\frac{3}{4} \div \frac{3}{4}$

4. In 1887, Frenchman Charles Wulff patented a balloon powered by birds. Dozens of birds in a cage flapped their wings to lift the balloon (carrying Wulff in a basket). How long ago was this?

5. Find the area of this helicopter landing pad.

Welcome to my pad.

1. A man named Henry Langer (nicknamed Cloudbuster Hen Langer) took a plane ride for the first time in 1932 and parachuted to the ground. After that, he took many more rides in airplanes, but never landed in one. He parachuted down every time. To find out how often Henry did this, you will have to solve the equation. Its answer (the variable **t**) will give you the number!

$$8,000 - 2t = 10t + 2,252$$

2. A paper airplane weighs 6.4 oz. How many grams does it weigh? *(Round to the nearest whole gram.)*

3. Compute: $\sqrt{625} - 72 =$

4. Correct the mistakes.

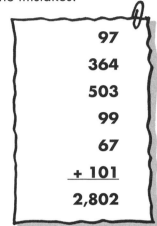

```
    97
   364
   503
    99
    67
 + 101
 2,802
```

5. Challenge Problem

Decorate each kite with a different repeating pattern.

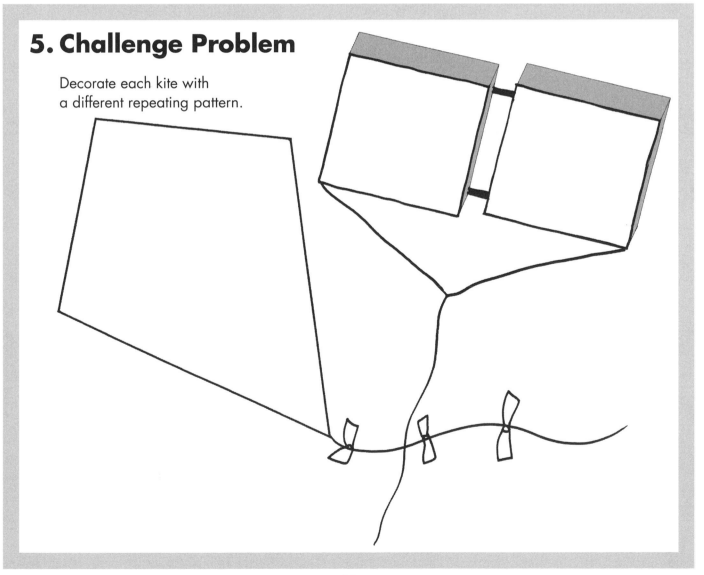

1. Which of these are integers?

○ $-7\frac{1}{2}$　　○ **45.05**　　○ **0**　　○ **-30**

○ **23.5**　　○ $\frac{1}{2}$　　○ **66**　　○ **-1000**

2. Will the number sentence below help to solve the problem?

A queen stood on the deck of her yacht, 30 feet above the sea. Her crown slipped and fell into the water, landing on a coral reef 12 feet below the water's surface. How far did it fall?

30 – (–12) =

Ooops!

3. Compute: **987 x 123 =**

4. Draw two real-life objects that are cylinders.

5. Solve the problem. Tell how you solved it.

A king is selecting jewels for his new crown from a black velvet bag. The bag contains twenty rubies, six diamonds, six sapphires, and eight emeralds. He reaches in and grabs one jewel. What are the odds against it being something other than a diamond?

1. Solve the equation.

(40y ÷ 2y) + 12 = 32

2. A meter is closest to

○ 3 yds　　○ $\frac{1}{2}$ mile

○ 3 ft　　　○ 20 in

○ 10 cm　　○ 1,000 cm

3. Compute:　**909.09 x 0.09 =**

4. Princess Bria has 5,000 nickels and 300 quarters. Princess Pia has 698 quarters, 1,500 dimes, and 6 nickels. Who has the most money?

5. King Lucas keeps his crown locked in this box. The inside measurements are shown. What is the volume of the box?

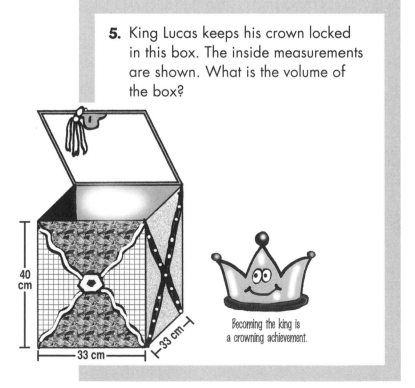

40 cm

33 cm

33 cm

Becoming the king is a crowning achievement.

1. Is this statement true or false?

A **combination** is an arrangement of objects in a particular order.

2. Compute: **−6,835 ÷ 1,367 + 1,000 =**

3. Write an equation to solve the problem.

Not long ago, Queen Elizabeth II of England celebrated the golden (50th) anniversary of her ascension to the throne. Prince Charles was born four years before she became queen. Prince Charles turned 50 in 1998. In what year did Elizabeth become queen?

4. How many vertices are found on a pyramid with a pentagonal base?

5. In 1977, Queen Elizabeth II traveled throughout the Commonwealth to share with the people the celebration of her 25th anniversary as queen. Her trip covered 56,000 miles in the year. Write and solve a proportion to find the number of miles she traveled (on average) in a three-month period.

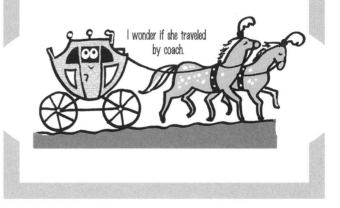

I wonder if she traveled by coach.

1. Write the first 15 positive composite numbers.

2. King Nebuchadnezzar II ruled in Mesopotamia from 605 BC to 562 BC. King Edgar ruled in England from 957 AD to 975 AD. Write a ratio that compares the length of Edgar's reign to Nebuchadnezzar's reign.

Let me think.

3. Compute: $11\frac{8}{10} - 6\frac{3}{5} =$

4. Is this solution correct?

$$50w ÷ (90 + w) = 20$$
$$W = 60$$

5. Queen Jessica had this large, circular platform built for her throne.
   a. What is the circumference?
   b. What is the area?

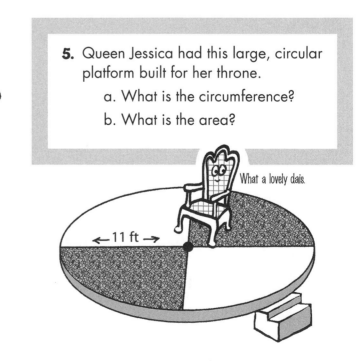

What a lovely dais.

←11 ft →

1. Compute: **(10 x 0.08) ÷ 4 =**

2. Find **m** if **n** = 30.

$$100m - n^2 - 2100 = 0$$

3. A bag of chess pieces holds six queens, three kings, two knights, and four pawns. Prince Edwin reaches into the dark bag and gets two pieces. What is the probability that he will draw out a pawn and a king?

4. Choose the best estimate:

61,037 x 1,205 x 27 =

a. 18,000,000,000

b. 1,800,000,000

c. 180,000,000

d. 18,000,000

e. 1,800,000

f. 180,000

5. Challenge Problem

Write these dates in standard notation.

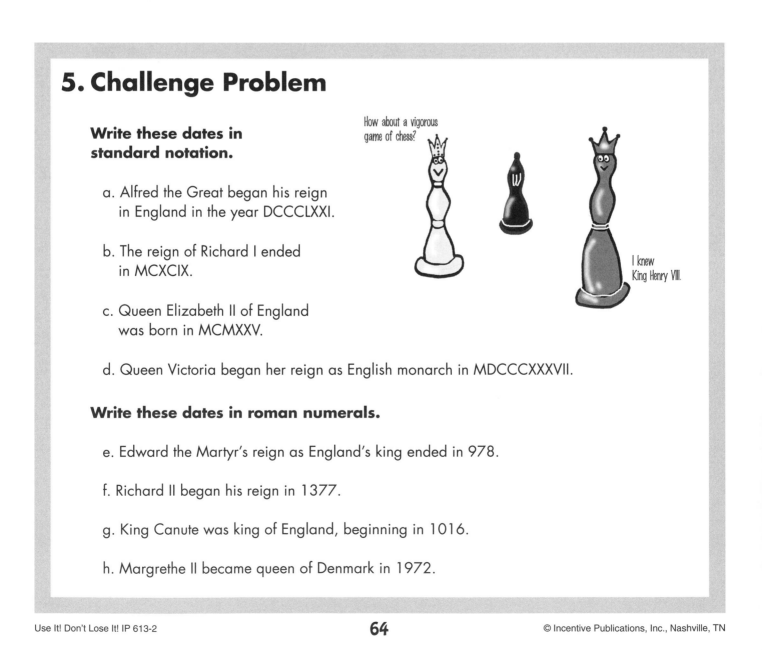

How about a vigorous game of chess?

I knew King Henry VIII.

a. Alfred the Great began his reign in England in the year DCCCLXXI.

b. The reign of Richard I ended in MCXCIX.

c. Queen Elizabeth II of England was born in MCMXXV.

d. Queen Victoria began her reign as English monarch in MDCCCXXXVII.

Write these dates in roman numerals.

e. Edward the Martyr's reign as England's king ended in 978.

f. Richard II began his reign in 1377.

g. King Canute was king of England, beginning in 1016.

h. Margrethe II became queen of Denmark in 1972.

1. Compute:

$$201,030,405$$
$$+ \; 310,909,466$$

2. A painter has six different colors of paint on his table. He mixes three colors together. How many different combinations of colors are possible?

3. Write the words to match the expression.

$$9c^3 - 20$$

4. Which angles are not congruent to **c**?

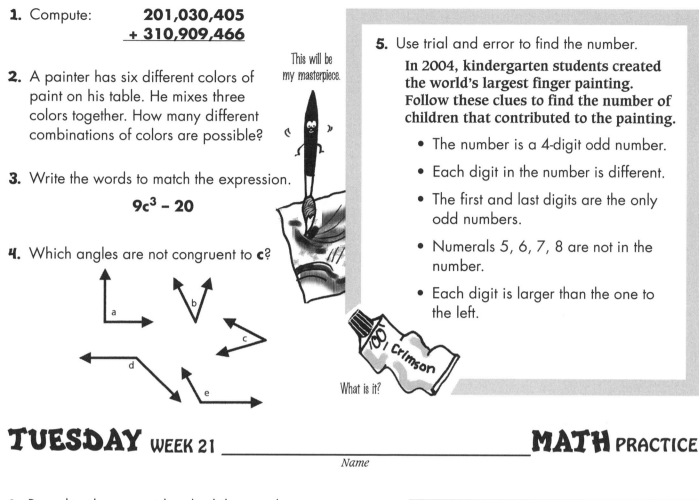

This will be my masterpiece.

What is it?

5. Use trial and error to find the number.

In 2004, kindergarten students created the world's largest finger painting. Follow these clues to find the number of children that contributed to the painting.

- The number is a 4-digit odd number.
- Each digit in the number is different.
- The first and last digits are the only odd numbers.
- Numerals 5, 6, 7, 8 are not in the number.
- Each digit is larger than the one to the left.

1. Round to the nearest hundred thousand.

10,962,475,199

2. Simplify.

$$2y^2 + y^2 + 5y - 16 = 52$$

3. Compute:

222.022 + 0.88 =

4. What do you need to know to determine the approximate area of the painter's palette?

I'm ready for a bigger palette.

5. Use mental math to find the approximate age to which each of these artists lived.

a. Van Gogh: 1853 – 1890

b. Monet: 1840 – 1926

c. Picasso: 1881 – 1973

d. O'Keefe: 1887 – 1986

e. Renoir: 1841 – 1919

f. Warhol: 1928 – 1987

1. Write a mathematical statement to match the words.

the sum of forty times a number (x) and fifty times the square of another number (y)

2. Define an **arc**.

3. Compute: **−5,000 x (−32) =**

4. Andy Warhol became famous for his *pop art* creations. One of his most talked-about paintings is titled **100 Soup Cans**. If Warhol used 0.15 lb of paint to paint each of the cans in the painting, how many ounces of paint would he have used?

I think my dad posed for that painting.

5. Maxine decides to make a painting by dropping blobs of paint at various locations on a coordinate grid. She creates a two-quadrant grid, complete with numbers on the **x** axis and **y** axis. The **x** axis is numbered from −20 to 20. The **y** axis is numbered from 0 to 35. Which of the following locations are possible for her paint blobs on this grid?

a. (−14, −20)　　e. (7, 30)
b. (29, 12)　　　f. (−10, 10)
c. (16, 33)　　　g. (−9, −25)
d. (−11, −31)　　h. (−4, 28)

1. Solve the problem. Explain how you solved it. Tell what operations you used.

Italian painter Botticelli painted *The Birth of Venus* **in 1483. How long ago was this?**

2. Compute: $4\frac{1}{5} \times 9\frac{3}{4} =$

3. Solve the equation.

66b = −33

4. Write this number in standard notation.

four hundred thirty thousand twenty-two

This painting is called, "Three Men On A Bus."

?

I don't get it!

5. This black and white painting is displayed in an art gallery. What is the area of the white portion?

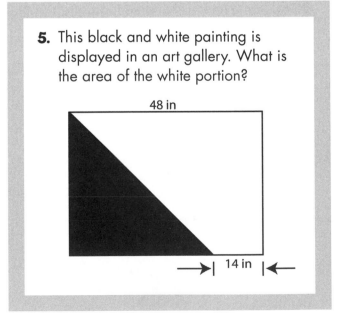

48 in

14 in

Name

1. Use the inverse operation to check the accuracy of the answer. Show your work.

$$4,080 \div 20 = 2,040$$

2. Which ordered pairs (x, y) are solutions to the equation below?

$$x = -y + 5$$

a. (3, –8)

b. (–3, 8)

c. (–6, 11)

d. (10, –5)

3. Compute:

$$\begin{array}{r} 1,200 \\ \times\ 60 \\ \hline \end{array}$$

4. A group of art students is making a sculpture out of coins. There are two bags of coins, each containing 1,000 quarters, 100 dimes, and 10 pennies. Al reaches into one bag to grab a coin. Sal reaches into the second bag to get a coin. What is the probability that both students will get a quarter?

Give the definition of **independent events**. Then tell if these are independent events (the two students getting one coin each).

This is great!

I can't wait to get started.

5. Challenge Problem

An artist has planned this wall mural design, and is now ready to purchase paint. Each jar of paint costs $2.50 and will cover 1.5 square feet. How much of each color will she need to buy, and what will the total cost be?

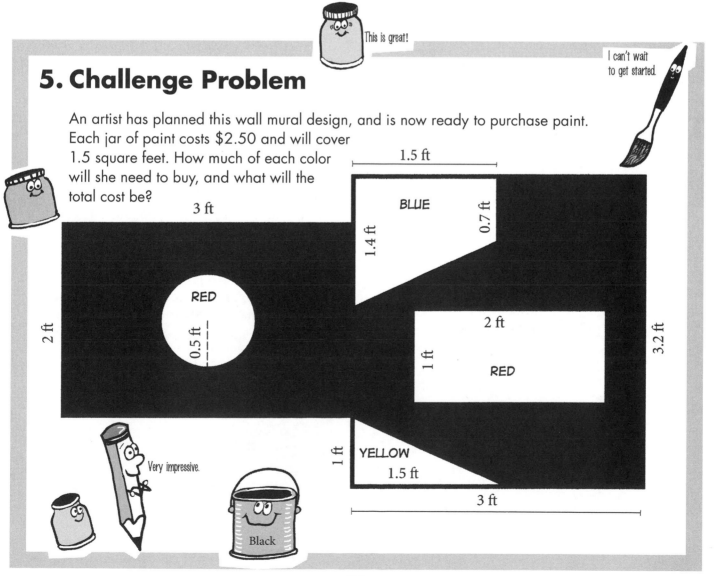

Very impressive.

Black

1. Believe it or not—someone paid $8,000 for Elvis Presley's sixth-grade report card! At the same auction, one of his keys sold for $23,000, and one of his capes brought in $85,000. If the same buyer took home all three items, what was the total bill?

What is Elvis's pencil worth?

2. Compute: $7\overline{)24,857}$

3. Write an equation to match the statement.

   The difference between one hundred twenty and five times a number (n) equals the number (n).

4. A pentagonal prism:
   a. the number of faces is _____
   b. the number of edges is _____
   c. the number of vertices is _____

   Draw a pentagonal prism.

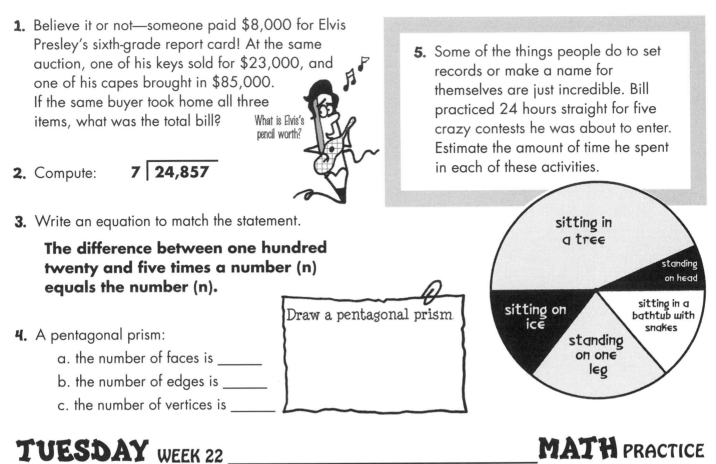

5. Some of the things people do to set records or make a name for themselves are just incredible. Bill practiced 24 hours straight for five crazy contests he was about to enter. Estimate the amount of time he spent in each of these activities.

- sitting in a tree
- standing on head
- sitting in a bathtub with snakes
- standing on one leg
- sitting on ice

1. Compute: **687.5 ÷ 55 =**

2. Susan Montgomery Williams, of Fresno, California, blew a record-breaking bubblegum bubble. The bubble had a diameter of 23.2 inches. The approximate volume of the bubble is

   ○ **6,535 in³**   ○ **1,560.9 in³**

   ○ **4,901.2 in³** ○ **19,605 in²**

3. It's amazing! Some snails have as many as 25,600 teeth in their tiny mouths. Write this number in expanded notation.

4. What number is the opposite of **−39.5**?

5. Choose the equation that will solve this problem.

   In 1917, a tornado traveled 293 miles through Illinois and Indiana in just seven hours. What was the tornado's rate in miles per minute?

   a. 1917 ÷ x = 293
   b. 293 x 60 = 7x
   c. x = 293/(7 x 60)
   d. x = 7(293 − 60)

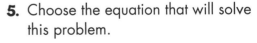

I won the cross-country race.

1. Which operation should be done second?

$$4b + 3(6b) - 16 + 4 = 98$$

2. Solve the problem. Tell how you solved it.

A Chicago candy company created a ten-pound gumdrop. It contained 15,127 calories! A mouse crept into the factory and ate a four-ounce piece. How many calories did he consume?

3. Compute: $62\overline{)-3,410}$

4. Which figures are right triangles?

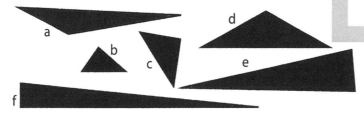

Measurement is my life.

5. Cross out the one you cannot compare and number the items in order of their length from shortest to longest.

UNBELIEVABLY LONG!

Record-Breaking Item	Length
Burrito	140 yd
Potato chip	25 in
Paper chain	29 mi
Kite	70 yd
Hot dog	3,001 ft
Necktie	326.9
Comic strip	100 yd

1. Which is greater?

$$6^5 \text{ or } 7^4$$

2. Solve the equation.

$$-86 + 5d^2 + 16 = 110$$

3. Compute: $\dfrac{6}{9} \div \dfrac{1}{4} =$

4. At the annual Chain Saw Chuck contest in Whitehorse, Yukon, Canada, someone hurled a chainsaw almost 55 feet. The competitor estimated that he had thrown the chainsaw over 50 meters. Is this a reasonable measurement?

5. Create a table to help solve this problem.

The Denver Mint (USA) produces 32 million pennies a day. A man with a metal detector found a total of 289,630 pennies and 4,000 dimes in a year. A fountain cleaner took 78,001 pennies, 2,000 quarters, 3,938 dimes, and 7,014 nickels out of a fountain. An armored car near Seattle lost 400,000 pennies when they fell out the back! What is the difference between the greatest and least amounts of money in these events?

1. Write a number sentence that shows the **associative property for multiplication.**

2. Find a pair of numbers (x, y) that makes this statement true.

$$\frac{10x}{2y} = -6$$

3. Compute: **6,060,606**
   – 2,808,088

4. Lil draws a piece of candy from a bag that has five root beer candies, six lime candies, and four cherry candies. At the same time, she flips a coin. What is the probability of her getting heads and a cherry candy?

We want candy – candy is dandy!

5. Challenge Problem

These are some fairly outrageous feats. Are the measurements reasonable? Write **yes** or **no** for each example.

____ **A.** Paul Warshauer and Paul Adler, students at a school in Illinois, built a house out of playing cards. The house was 50 "stories" (cards) high and contained 7,725 cards. Is 120,000 ft² a reasonable estimate of the outside surface area of the structure?

____ **B.** A 71-pound turkey (named "Mr. Chuckie") was sold at an auction for $2,000. Could the buyer have paid for the purchase with 15 bills?

____ **C.** The famous baseball player Ty Cobb is said to have walked 30 miles each winter day with lead in his shoes. At this rate, could he have walked 2,100 miles in a winter?

____ **D.** There is a 168,000 square mile area in Australia that is patrolled by police officers mounted on camels! Could the perimeter measure 1,640 miles?

____ **E.** A team of people from Pennsylvania pushed a hospital bed 1,776 miles in 17 days. At this rate, could they cover 10,000 miles in a month?

____ **F.** When Skylar Dae Westerholm was born in 1992, she was the first female to be born into the Westerholm family of North Dakota in 110 years. Was the last female born in 1882?

Name

1. There are over 37,000 different species of arachnids. Only 25 are poisonous to humans. Write a ratio in the form of a fraction to compare the number of poisonous species to the total number of arachnid species.

2. Are the terms like or unlike?

   $n + 3n^2 + 5n^3$

3. There are 2,648 spiders in my basement. Compute the number of legs.

4. Name this figure.

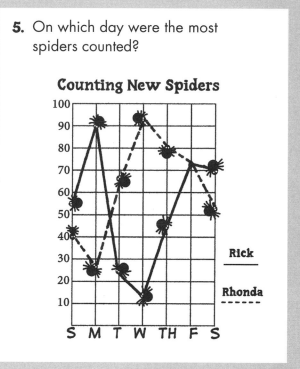

We're counting on you to figure this out.

5. On which day were the most spiders counted?

Counting New Spiders

Rick ———
Rhonda - - - -

Name

1. Some scientists recorded the names of thirty-seven thousand nineteen spider species. Write this number in standard notation.

2. Write the next three numbers.

   1.4092; 4.0921; 0.9214;

   _____, _____, _____

I hope you don't have arachniphobia.

3. Compute: **5.63 x 0.66 =**

4. Find the surface area of a rectangular prism with the dimensions 12 cm by 9 cm by 4 cm.

5. Choose the correct answer.

   The South American Bird-eating Spider is the largest spider in the world. Its leg can span up to 11 inches. Assume that when the spider's legs are stretched out, they are equidistant.
   If you drew a circle around the outside edge, what would be the approximate perimeter?

   a. 34.54 in   c. 14.1 in
   b. 69.08 in   d. 40 in

I'm going in circles.

WEDNESDAY WEEK 23 _____ MATH PRACTICE

Name

1. Compute: $-600 - (-3,700) - 100 =$

2. There are three brown spiders, six black spiders, and two red spiders in my drawer. Two find their way into the trap. What are the possible outcomes for which two get trapped?

I have a lot of relatives.

3. Simplify the equation.

   $m + 5 = n - 7$

4. Four angles in a pentagon measure 88°, 72°, 72°, and 60°. What is the measure of the last angle?

5. Which arachnids has Julia seen more than twice as often as the orb weaver?

Arachnids Julia Has Seen

Kind	Number	Kind	Number
Tarantula	14	Funnel web	7
Black widow	2	House	146
Purse web	3	Orange garden	6
Daddy-longlegs	80	Cellar	22
Fisher	12	Orb weaver	11
Grasshopper	23	Scorpion	8

THURSDAY WEEK 23 _____ MATH PRACTICE

Name

1. Round to the nearest ten.

   $384 \frac{2}{5}$

2. The temperature inside an old attic was 99°F. Give the formula that can be used to convert this into a Celsius temperature. Then find the Celsius temperature.

3. Compute: $\frac{7}{20} - \frac{3}{5} =$

4. Solve the equation.

   $6p \div 60 = -5$

5. Add up the total points for the spiders!

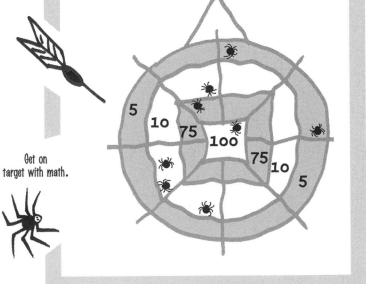

Get on target with math.

5   10   75   100   75   10   5

72

1. Give the answer to this problem in standard notation. Explain how you solved the problem.

$$2.9 \times 10^6 - 3.6 \times 10^4 =$$

2. **336** is 56% of what number?

3. Which solution is correct?

−20g + 12 = 118

    a. g = 5.3   b. g = 6.5   c. g = −5.3

4. Find the mistakes and give the correct answer.

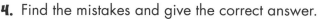

```
        8,261
    x     234
       33044
       23783
    + 16422
    1,923,174
```

5. Challenge Problem

Survey 50 people (or as close to 50 as you can get). Ask each one which of the animals on the list inspires the most fear for them. Use the table (list) as a tally sheet. Then display the data you collect in the form of a circle graph. Give the graph a title.

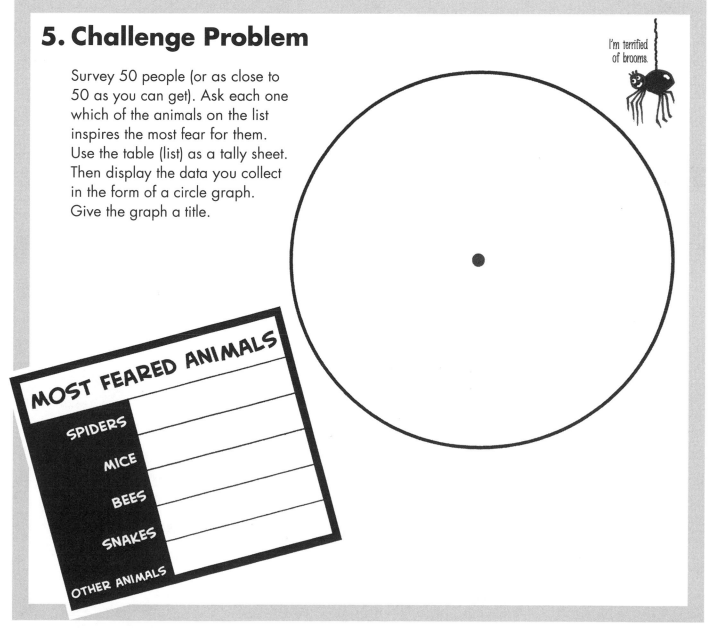

I'm terrified of brooms.

MOST FEARED ANIMALS

SPIDERS

MICE

BEES

SNAKES

OTHER ANIMALS

1. The Okefenokee Swamp in southeastern Georgia and northeastern Florida is about 48 km wide and 60 km long. What is its area?

2. Which operation should be done first?

    596 + 402 – 36 =

3. There are six alligators and eight crocodiles in the channel behind Greg's house. There are equal numbers of males and females of each animal. Two crawl out onto the bank. What is the probability that both are females?

4. Which figure is similar to the first (a)?

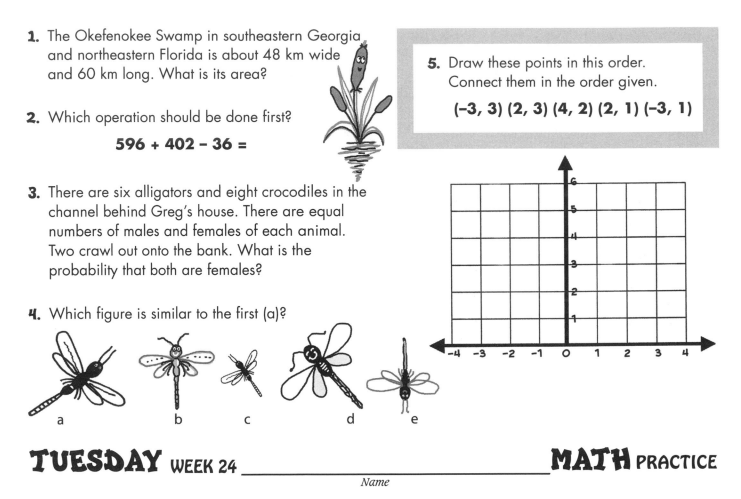

a   b   c   d   e

5. Draw these points in this order. Connect them in the order given.

    (–3, 3) (2, 3) (4, 2) (2, 1) (–3, 1)

1. Which places have a zero value in this number?

    20,064,602,019

2. A crocodile's weight is only about $\frac{2}{3}$ of the weight of an average American alligator. The alligator in the Hansen's swimming pool weighs 72 pounds. A crocodile of similar size would weigh

    ○ **48 lb**   ○ **96 lb**

    ○ **108 lb**   ○ **24 lb**

3. Compute:

    $2,451.12 ÷ 56 =

4. Solve the equation.

    12x – 100 = 2x – 20

Is biting allowed?

5. Alphonso won $3,375 last year in prize money from alligator-wrestling matches. He earned an average of $120 for each match. He won $715 from the 13 crocodile-riding exhibitions in which he participated.

    a. In how many alligator-wrestling matches did he participate?

    b. What was the average amount he earned for each crocodile-riding event?

1. Compute: 70 − (−20) + (−10) + (−40) =

2. Find the mean of these lengths.

11.5 kg   **9 kg**   **7.6 kg**

8.3 kg   **5.8 kg**

3. Fill in the missing symbol >, <, or =.

$4y^2 + 30$ ☐ $y^2 - 12$

4. Draw a triangular prism.
Tell which of the following
are true of this figure.

  a. It has nine edges.

  b. It has four faces.

  c. It has one square face.

  d. It has six vertices.

Triangular prism:

5. Put the baby alligators in order from
least to greatest lengths.

  Alligator A – 990 mm

  Alligator B – 0.4 m

  Alligator C – 8 in

  Alligator D – 26 in

  Alligator E – 29 cm

  Alligator F – 90 cm

Where's Momma?

She's probably hiding.

1. Simplify the expression:

7k + 9(k + 6) − 3k − 12

It's my birthday!

2. A newly hatched crocodile
baby was 9 inches long.
Within a year, he had grown
to a length of 7 feet. Is the
rate of his growth closer to
6 or 8 inches per month?

3. What is the greatest common
factor of **15** and **160**?

4. Compute:

$5\frac{2}{3} \times 9\frac{1}{5} =$

5. a. Write the formula for finding the
volume of a cylinder.

  b. The volume of a drum of water
that is four feet tall and two feet
in diameter is

    a. 50 ft^3

    b. 25 ft^3

    c. 13 ft^3

    d. 100 ft^3

1. Compute: **275,000 ÷ 250 =**

a. 3,000   c. 110

b. 11,000   d. 1,100

2. Fill in the missing operation.

$$650 - \boxed{} - 20 = -100$$

3. Simplify the equation.

$$7d^2 + 20d - d + 40 = 106$$

4. The Everglades Swamp is full of a strong, high grass called sawgrass. The height in inches of the tallest sawgrass is a number that fits these clues. What number(s) could it be?

Clues: This is a three-digit even number, all of whose digits are less than five. The first digit is smaller than the others, and the two even digits are the same. The sum of the digits is less than ten.

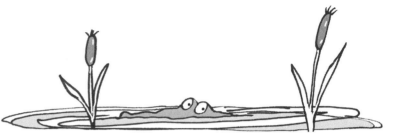

5. Challenge Problem

Four neighbors live in the only four houses in the swamp. The houses are in a line, beginning with number 20. Each neighbor has a different pet and each has a different profession. Follow the clues to find out: **Who owns the alligator?**

- The crocodile owner lives next to Charlie.

- Tonya is not an accountant.

- Charlie is a teacher.

- The accountant lives at one end of the row.

- Tonya's pet is a python.

- The crocodile owner lives next to the hippopotamus owner.

- The owner of the alligator lives between the teacher and the artist.

- Angie is not a chef.

- The lowest-numbered house belongs to Angie.

- The chef lives next to the python owner.

- Max lives next door to an artist.

MONDAY WEEK 25 _____ MATH PRACTICE

Name

1. Correct the mistakes.

286,034 + 195,686 = 190,458

It must be beautiful in these caverns.

2. Estimate the answer.

Strange, eyeless fish live in Echo River (found inside Mammoth Cave). If there are three fish for each nine cubic feet of water, how many would be found in a section of the river 60 ft long, 30 ft wide, and 15 ft deep?

3. Write an algebraic expression for the phrase:

four flashlights fewer than a number (x)

4. This space figure has been cut open and flattened. What figure is it?

5. Find the median of these stalagmite heights.

WORLD'S LARGEST STALAGMITES		
CAVE LOCATION	COUNTY	HEIGHT
Roznava Cave	Slovakia	32 m
Mammoth Cave	USA	19 m
Zhi Jin Cave	China	67.2 m
Slaughter Canyon Cave	USA	27 m
Grotto Ispinigoli	Italy	38 m

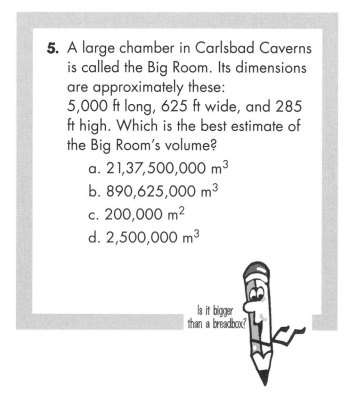

TUESDAY WEEK 25 _____ MATH PRACTICE

Name

1. Write five fractions that are $< \frac{3}{7}$. Do not repeat the same denominator.

2. Compute:

Find the difference between seventy and seventy-seven hundredths and thirty-nine thousandths.

3. Find the value of the expression if y = 12.

$$6y^2 - 520$$

4. Find the area of this figure.

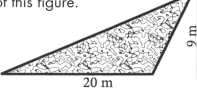

9 m

20 m

5. A large chamber in Carlsbad Caverns is called the Big Room. Its dimensions are approximately these: 5,000 ft long, 625 ft wide, and 285 ft high. Which is the best estimate of the Big Room's volume?

    a. 21,37,500,000 m³
    b. 890,625,000 m³
    c. 200,000 m²
    d. 2,500,000 m³

Is it bigger than a breadbox?

1. A box holds raincoats for cave visitors. There are 35 yellow coats, 12 red coats, 10 green coats, and 3 black coats. Jon grabs two coats from the box. What is the probability that he'll get two red coats?

Sometimes I'm all wet.

2. Compute: **−2,000 x 39.5 =**

3. Some friends hiked six straight days in the Mammoth Cave system. They hiked 2.6 mi on Monday, 2.9 mi on Tuesday, and 3.2 mi on Wednesday. Predict the distance they will hike on Saturday.

4. How many lines of symmetry can be drawn through this figure?

5. Is the equation a good choice for solving this problem?

Caving (the recreational sport of exploring caves) is an adventure that is growing in popularity. When Anne, Dan, and Stan added up the individual times they had spent in caves, the total came to 12,000 hours. Anne spent twice as many hours caving as Stan and Dan together. Dan and Stan found that they had spent exactly the same amount of time. How much time did Dan spend caving?

2s + s + s = 1,200

1. Gouffre de la Pierre St. Martin is one of the world's deepest caves—1.6 km Lou and Sue explore the cave to a depth of 800 meters. Write a ratio showing the comparison of this to the total depth of the cave.

Deep!

2. Compute: $\frac{2}{3}$ x $\frac{4}{5}$ =

3. Which object of caving equipment would weigh about two grams?

○ helmet ○ adult boots ○ bottle of water

○ Band-Aids ○ energy bar ○ flashlight

○ batteries ○ raincoat ○ ropes

4. If x = −5, what is y?

10x + 3y = −5

5. Granny Bantle hiked through Angel's Cave on March 23, 1996. At the time, she was 72 years, 5 months old. In what month and year was Granny born?

MONTH:			YEAR:			
DAY:						
1	2	3	4	5	6	7
8	9	10	11	12	13	14
15	16	17	18	19	20	21
22	23	24	25	26	27	28
29	30	31				

Write your answers here.

1. Estimate the quotient.

one hundred sixty-two thousand divided by seventy-five

2. The total measurement of a pair of two supplementary angles is

○ 360°   ○ 45°

○ 90°   ○ 180°

3. Compute:

7(900 + 15,000 – 2,000) =

4. What is the value of the expression if n = –10?

5n² + n – 250

a. –240   c. –760

b. 240   d. 760

5. Challenge Problem

Four cavers hike single file through the cave. Their names are Zach, Anna, Carly, and Sam. How many different permutations are there for this group of hikers?

Write all the possibilities, using the first letters of the names (Z, A, C, S).

PERMUTATIONS

1. A hummingbird performs an amazing feat many times a day. This tiny bird can beat its wings about 100 times a minute. How long would it take for the hummingbird to beat its wings 26,500 times?

This flapping is amazing – but tiring.

2. Compute: $53\overline{)48,760}$

3. Each composite number between 0 and 20 is written on a piece of paper and placed into a box. One paper is drawn. How many different outcomes are possible?

4. Draw a turn of this figure.

5. Which equation will solve the problem?

In its lifetime, a shark loses and grows back as many as 24,000 teeth. A group of beachcombers collects shark teeth on the beach. They find about 1,500 a year. How long will it take them to collect the teeth one shark grows in a lifetime?

a. $\dfrac{1500}{1} = \dfrac{24,000}{x}$

b. $\dfrac{1500}{24,000} = \dfrac{x}{12}$

c. $24,000x = 1,500$

1. An albatross can fly along at 25 mph—while it sleeps! If the sleeping bird covers 18.3 miles asleep, how long is her nap?

2. Compute: $23.8 \div 6.8 =$

3. Solve the equation.

$250 = 9x - 38$

4. Write four fractions that are equivalent to $\frac{6}{9}$.

I'll order more dog food.

5. Fido's owner buys small packages of treats for the dog. Each package holds 75 in³ of food. Will four packages of these treats fit into Fido's new dish (without being heaped above the top edge of the dish)?

I'm empty.

5 in

3 in   Fido

1. Evaluate the expression with n = –3 and m = 15.

$$4n - (-6) + m$$

2. A termite colony can eat 1,000 pounds of wood in a year! How much can it consume in a week? (Round to the nearest hundredth pound.)

3. Fill in the missing number.

$$(-70 + 100) \div \boxed{} = -5$$

4. Charlie drew an irregular hexagon. The total of the measures of five of the angles is 595°. What is the measure of the sixth angle?

I'm looking for a good table to eat.

Termites eat paper, too.

5. Which insect number, when compared to the number of beetles, results in a ratio of $\frac{3}{10}$?

Numbers of Known Species	
Number of Species	Insect
400,000	Beetles
165,000	Butterflies, moths
140,000	Ants, bees, wasps
120,000	Flies
90,000	Cicadas

1. Compute:

$$10\frac{2}{5} + 13\frac{1}{3} =$$

2. Which tool is best for measuring the amount of food a buffalo can eat in a day?

- ○ scale
- ○ ruler
- ○ odometer
- ○ quart jar
- ○ calendar
- ○ thermometer

3. Use words to write this number: **30.0203**

4. Which number pairs will solve this equation?

$$5x - y = 2$$

(3, 13) (1, 3) (–4, –20) (–2, 12)

5. Use mental math to arrive at an estimated solution to the problem.

The male sand grouse flies 50 miles (each way) to soak in water so that he can carry it back to his offspring. They drink the water held in his feathers. If he does this every other day for five weeks, How far will he fly?

I don't want to grouse, Dad, but I'm thirsty.

1. Which shows the identity property?

    a. $\frac{1}{2} + 0 = 0 + \frac{1}{2}$

    b. $92.5 \times 0 = 0$

    c. $-55 + 1 + 4 = 1 + 4 + (-55)$

    d. $1 \times 72 = 72$

2. Simplify the equation

$$\frac{6x + 12}{3} + 5x = 60$$

3. Is this computation correct?

$$565 \times 131 = 74{,}015$$

4. The median of a set of data is

    a. the difference between the greatest and least values in the data

    b. the item that occurs with the greatest frequency

    c. the sum of all the data divided by the number of data items

    d. the middle value when data items are arranged in numerical order

    e. the number of times an item of data occurs in the set

5. Challenge Problem

How many triangles are in this figure?

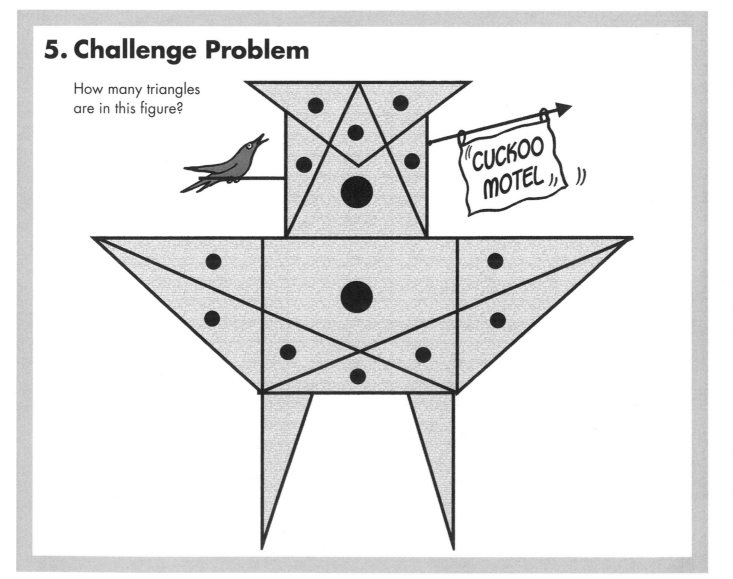

1. A bookshelf contains 30 biographies, 12 other nonfiction books, and 16 books of fiction. Someone hands Carly a book from the shelf. What is the probability that it is a biography?

2. Simplify the equation.

   $$\frac{30b}{6} + 40 = 13b$$

3. Members of the Parker family checked out 40 biographies from the library. Mom read $\frac{1}{4}$ of them, Dad read $\frac{1}{8}$ of them, and Dave read $\frac{3}{8}$ of the books. How many did Jana read?

4. Draw an irregular pentagon.

5. Some friends collect autographs of celebrities. They compare their collections. What is the average number of autographs for each member of this group of friends?

   Andy has 29

   Brad has 26

   Dana has 64

   Evan has 72

   Georgia has 35

   Tyrone has 51

   Juan has 19

   Kim has 40

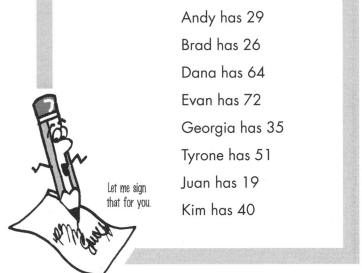

Let me sign that for you.

1. Jennifer Capriati was 14 when she played her first tennis match at Wimbledon, making her the youngest woman ever to play in this tournament. The year was 1990. In what year was Jennifer born?

This is easy. I can do it in my head.

2. Compute: **40.002 x 0.44 =**

3. Round to the nearest ten thousandth.

   100.032487

4. An input – output rule is **x = –2y**. If **y = –6**, what is **x**?

5. Alicia Keys has won nine Grammy Awards for her singing and songwriting. Millions of her CDs have sold around the world. Measure this to find the circumference of a CD.

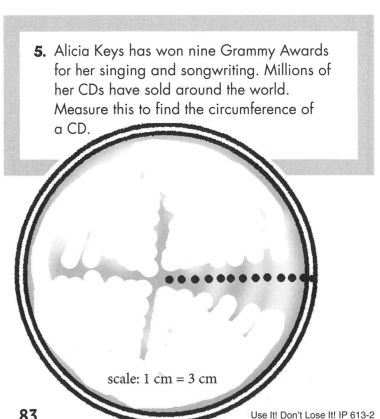

scale: 1 cm = 3 cm

1. Tom Brady, quarterback for the New England Patriots football team, led his team to three Super Bowl championships in four years. At this rate, how long would it take him to earn 12 wins?

2. Compute: **−20 + (−37) =**

3. JoAnn Barnes could swing 68 hula hoops around her body at the same time. Assume she has hula hoops of these colors: blue, green, red, yellow, and orange. If she wanted to swing only two colors at once, how many different color combinations are possible?

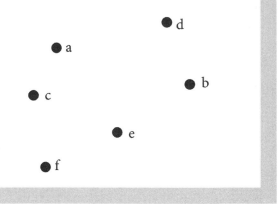
I hula hoop for fun.

4. Solve the equation.

   20 = m + 4/9

5. A. Draw a line segment from A to D.

   B. Draw a ray beginning at B and going through C.

   C. Draw a line that passes through E and F.

   D. Draw a line perpendicular to line EF.

   •d
   •a
   •c
   •b
   •e
   •f

1. Jean Blondin was the first person to cross Niagara Falls on a tightrope. He did this on June 30, 1859. The tenth person to accomplish this same feat did so on July 1, 1896. How many months between the two events?

Next time I'll try a tightwalk.

2. Write each fraction in lowest terms.

   a. $\frac{12}{15}$ c. $\frac{9}{27}$

   b. $\frac{17}{2}$ d. $\frac{16}{6}$

3. Compute: $\frac{8}{9} \times \frac{2}{3} =$

4. Draw the graph of ≥ −3.

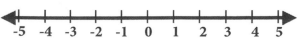
-5 -4 -3 -2 -1 0 1 2 3 4 5

5. Solve the problem. Tell how you arrived at the solution.

   Elvis Presley, with 127 hit songs, has the most top-selling hit songs of any U.S. singer. Write a percentage to show the comparison of these other singers to Elvis.

   a. Ray Charles – 72 hits

   b. Elton John – 59 hits

   c. Neil Diamond – 55 hits

   d. Aretha Franklin – 70 hits

   e. Barbra Streisand – 34 hits

1. Fill in the missing operation.

$$\frac{4}{7} \ \Box \ \frac{4}{5} = \frac{5}{7}$$

2. What is the difference between two hundred fifty-three and eighty-six?

3. Solve the equation. Write an explanation telling how you solved it.

$$-15x + 30 = x - 50$$

4. a. What is the mode in a set of statistical data?

b. What is the mode in this set of data?

12	9	30	35	40	33
26	10	35	34	36	30
35	13	31	35	39	29
40	35	17	22	50	31

5. Challenge Problem

Use trial and error to find the number that matches each set of clues.

You'll flip over these statistics!

a. the number of medals skateboarder Tony Hawk has won at X-Games:
a two-digit, odd number; sum of the digits is 6, number is <30

b. the year that Michelle Kwan skated in her first World Championship event:
an even number; two digits the same; sum of the digits is 23

c. the number of points Michael Jordan scored in his NBA career:
a five-digit, even number < 50,000; thousands, hundreds, and one digits are the same; one digit is 9; other digits are < 4

d. the number of years Nelson Mandela spent in prison:
a two-digit, odd number; sum of digits is 7; both digits < 7; first digit < second digit; difference between digits is 3

e. number of hours pilot Stephen Fosset flew without stopping:
a four-digit, even number; multiple of 100; sum of digits is 5; first digit < second; number is >1,450

1. Compute: **98,765 x 42 =**

2. Eighteen of the U.S. states border the Atlantic or Pacific Ocean. What percent of the states do not have an ocean border?

3. Which operation should be done last when solving this equation?

$$73 + 6(5 - x) - 55 = 300$$

4. Sara picks a USA state name at random. What are the odds in favor of the result being a state whose name begins with *North* or *New*?

How will I ever get to Boise?

Boise or Bust

5. Identify these properties of a circle:

   a. Name two central angles.

   b. Name two radii.

   c. Name a chord that is not a diameter.

   d. Name a tangent.

1. The 2000 U.S. census counted 50,500 Americans over the age of 100. It is estimated that there will be 834,000 over 100 by the year 2050. What is the percent of increase?

   1,550%   **165%**

   0%   **150%**   **15.5%**

We love birthdays!

2. Write this number in scientific notation.

   374,000,000

3. Use words to write this equation.

   4(10−y) = −8

4. Compute: **$356.39 x 12 =**

5. The Gateway Arch in St. Louis, MO is the tallest monument constructed in the United States. Measure the picture to find the arch's height at the highest point.

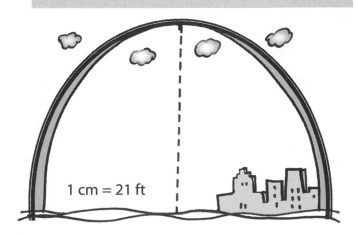

1 cm = 21 ft

1. How many vertices can be found on a pyramid with an octagonal base?

16   12   9   10   8

2. Compute: **–20 x (–4) x (–6) =**

3. What number has the opposite value from **–35**?

4. Solve this problem to find the number of parks, monuments, and recreational areas within the U.S. National Park System as of the end of the 2003 NBA season.

$$12^2 + 15^2 + \sqrt{324} + 1 =$$

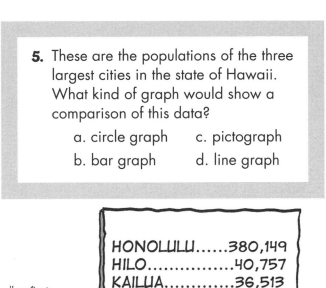

5. These are the populations of the three largest cities in the state of Hawaii. What kind of graph would show a comparison of this data?

   a. circle graph   c. pictograph
   b. bar graph   d. line graph

I'm sailing to the Big Island.

HONOLULU......380,149
HILO...............40,757
KAILUA............36,513

1. Solve the equation.

$$-3y = -40 + 4$$

2. Write this as a fraction, decimal, and percent.

   eighteen hundredths

3. Compute: $10\frac{2}{3} \div 2\frac{5}{6} =$

4. The measure of angle A is closest to

   ○ 205°   ○ 130°
   ○ 45°   ○ 175°
   ○ 60°   ○ 95°

A

5. Solve the problem. Tell how you solved it.

The population of Alaska is 655,435. Rhode Island has 153,767 more people than Montana. Vermont has 149,489 fewer than South Dakota. Montana has 155,982 more people than South Dakota. Alaska has 425,197 fewer people than Rhode Island. Which state has a larger population: Alaska or Vermont?

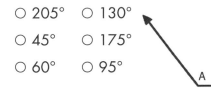

U.S.A. State Populations

1. Compute:

$$860,000 \div 430 =$$

- ○ 20
- ○ 20,000
- ○ 2,000,000
- ○ 20
- ○ 2,000
- ○ 200,000

2. Simplify the expression.

$$3^2 + 6x - 7x + 20$$

3. Compute:

$$1,000 + 505 - (100 + 43) =$$

4. Which proportion will solve the problem?

The Biscayne National Park in eastern Florida covers 270 square miles. In all, 95 percent of the park is underwater. What amount of park space is not underwater?

a. $\dfrac{x}{270} = \dfrac{95}{100}$

b. $\dfrac{95}{270} = \dfrac{x}{100}$

c. $\dfrac{270}{x} = \dfrac{95}{100}$

---

5. Challenge Problem

The 2000 U.S. census measured the United States population to be 281,421,906 people.

a. 49.1 percent of the population at that time was male. How many females were counted?

b. 3.6 percent of the population was Asian, Native Hawaiian, or Pacific Islander. How many people was this? (Round to the nearest whole number.)

c. Life expectancy (in 2000) had increased to 74.4 years from 47.3 years in 1900. What is the percent of increase?

d. About 14.5 percent of the population was made up of kids from ages 5 to 14. How many kids were there in this age group?

e. Visit the pop clock on the web to find out the current (up-to-the-minute) U.S. population estimate. Compare this to the 2000 census figure. www.census.gov/main/www/popclock.html

88

1. Find the surface area of this figure.

4 in

8 in

2. The first time the U.S. Supreme Court found a U.S. law unconstitutional was in the year 1803. How long ago was this?

3. Compute: $44,044,004$
$$- 303,330$$

5. The county clerk ordered robes for all the county judges. When the box of 2,000 robes came, she took out 40 robes and checked them over. Out of this sample, she found that six had broken zippers. How many robes in the whole box could she expect to have broken zippers?

4. Draw the figure that would come next.

1. Compute: $406 - 26.047 =$

2. Write this equation.

Twice a number (x) added to the sum of the number (x) and ten is equal to thirty-seven.

I broke a mathematical law.

3. 36 inches = _____ centimeters
  a. 36   c. 14.2
  b. 91.4   d. 100

4. A court settlement for damage to a fire hydrant cost Mr. McGroo $266. He has 915 quarters and 360 dimes. Is this enough to pay the fine?

5. How much time passed between the most recent and the earliest laws described?

Year	Place	Law
1785	France	All handkerchiefs must be square.
330 B.C.	Greece	Children must care for their aged parents.
1807	Russia	Men cannot wear long pants.
1610	Virginia, USA	No one can miss church more than three times in a row.
1872	California, USA	It is forbidden to disturb birds nesting in a cemetery.
1951	Burma	Crossword puzzles are banned.

1. Draw a figure that is congruent to this figure.

2. A jury is making a decision about what award to give to a woman in a personal injury lawsuit. The judge tells them that they can give any amount that is zero or any multiple of $100 up to $15,500. How many possible outcomes are there for the jury to consider?

Whoa, another big number.

3. Solve the equation.

$$3(15y - 9) - 24y = 15$$

4. Compute: **−82 x 300 + 50 =**

5. Draw a flip of the figure in the right-hand quadrant of the grid.

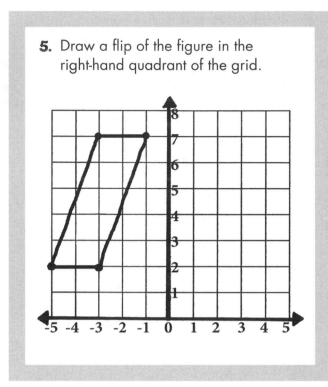

1. A funny law in Piqua, Ohio sets a time before which people cannot take baths. To find the time, write the smallest four-digit number possible.

__ __ : __ __ **pm**

2. Simplify the equation.

$$9(w + 4) + \frac{20}{4} - 3w = 71$$

It's criminal!

3. Compute: $\frac{85}{9} + \frac{14}{15} =$

4. A judge read the surprising will of G. Clifford Pruet. The document required that $400,000 be spent on clothing for animals. If 36 cats and 44 dogs were clothed, how much money would be spent on each one?

5. Lucas LaRose claimed that Mrs. Perry's dog had destroyed his flower garden. The courts required Mrs. Perry to pay $35 per square foot for the damaged garden. How much did she have to pay?

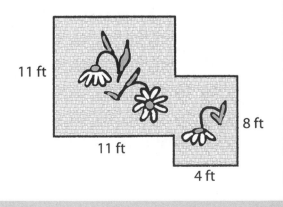

11 ft

11 ft

8 ft

4 ft

1. Is the computation correct?

$$\begin{array}{r} 666 \text{ R } 6 \\ 25 \overline{)16,654} \end{array}$$

2. Which operation should be done last?

$$13x - 7x + 6^2 = 96$$

3. Use symbols and numbers to write this expression.

the product of thirty and nineteen times a number (b)

4. The longest trial on record took place in New Delhi, India. The trial lasted 33 years and cost $677,000. The cost of the trial per month was closest to

  a. $170.00

  b. $56,400.00

  c. $1,710.00

  d. $20,500.00

  e. $2,052.00

What is your judgment about these cases?

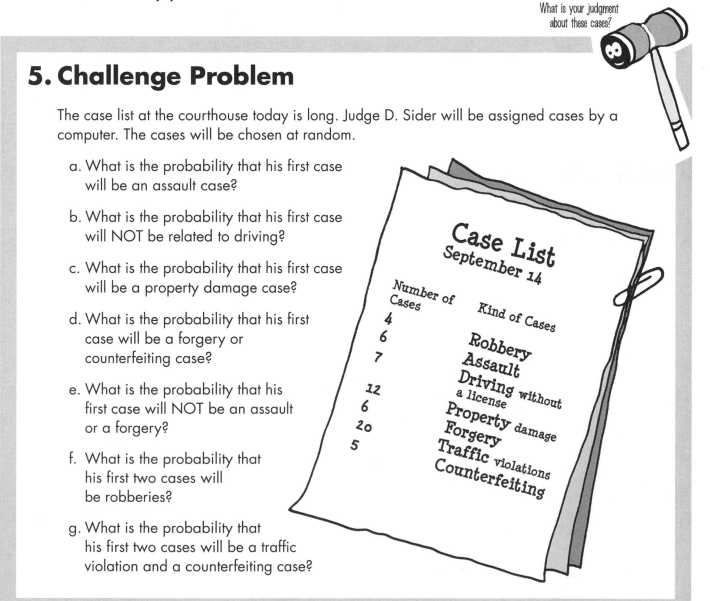

5. Challenge Problem

The case list at the courthouse today is long. Judge D. Sider will be assigned cases by a computer. The cases will be chosen at random.

  a. What is the probability that his first case will be an assault case?

  b. What is the probability that his first case will NOT be related to driving?

  c. What is the probability that his first case will be a property damage case?

  d. What is the probability that his first case will be a forgery or counterfeiting case?

  e. What is the probability that his first case will NOT be an assault or a forgery?

  f. What is the probability that his first two cases will be robberies?

  g. What is the probability that his first two cases will be a traffic violation and a counterfeiting case?

Case List
September 14

Number of Cases	Kind of Cases
4	Robbery
6	Assault
7	Driving without a license
12	Property damage
6	Forgery
20	Traffic violations
5	Counterfeiting

1. Use the inverse operation to check this calculation.

24,396 ÷ 76 = 321

2. At a café that specializes in chocolate, there are 91 ounces of chocolate powder in 13 cups of hot chocolate. How many cups can be made with 385 ounces?

3. Is the solution correct?

6p – 4(p + 5) = 38
p = 29

4. A triangle has a 35° angle and a 65° angle. What is the measure of the third angle?

Just the essentials.

5. a. Find the mode of the data.

b. Find the median of the data.

c. Find the mean of the data.

d. Find the range of the data.

Restaurant Supplies
Plates........................$6.50 ea
Candle Holder.............$7.00
Sugar Shaker...............$3.90
Tablecloth...................$15.50
French Fry Slicer........$28.60
Cream Pitcher.............$4.20
Salt & Pepper Shaker...$3.90
Coffee Mug.................$4.50

1. What are the variables in this expression?

5c + 8d – d² + c

2. Write a problem related to a restaurant. The problem must have an answer of –$5,100.

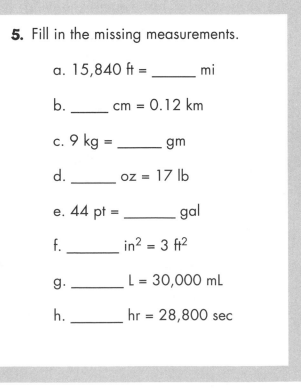

It's the math problem du jour.

3. Compute:

5.7 | 1.881

4. Which numbers are not divisible by six?

○ 270   ○ 76   ○ 640

○ 144   ○ 206   ○ 700

5. Fill in the missing measurements.

a. 15,840 ft = _____ mi

b. _____ cm = 0.12 km

c. 9 kg = _____ gm

d. _____ oz = 17 lb

e. 44 pt = _____ gal

f. _____ in² = 3 ft²

g. _____ L = 30,000 mL

h. _____ hr = 28,800 sec

1. Underline any information that is not needed to solve the problem.

> **The building that houses Lynn's Paradise Café in Louisville, Kentucky is decorated with an 8-foot by 24-foot mural made of corn cobs. The café is open 15 hours on Tuesday through Friday, and a total of 26 hours on the weekend. What is the area covered by the mural?**

2. Compute: **−3,696 ÷ 44 =**

3. Solve the equation:

> **A number (q) is equal to nine times the difference between the number (q) and negative six.**

4. A figure has six faces, twelve edges, and eight vertices. What is the figure?

5. At Hank's café, Hank gives a sandwich and drink of his choice to each customer. The drinks are tea, coffee, and milk. The sandwiches are turkey, roast beef, ham, and chicken salad. Finish the tree diagram to show the possible combinations that a customer might be given.

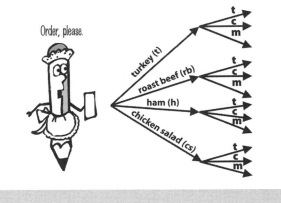

1. Compute: $\frac{2}{5} \times \frac{1}{2} \times \frac{3}{9} =$

2. A diner orders deep-fried caterpillars every time he comes into Joe's Eatery. He eats 4 on Mondays, 7 on Tuesdays, 13 on Wednesdays, and 25 on Thursdays. Predict the number he eats on Saturdays.

3. Simplify the expression.

$5(a^2 + a - 7) + 6c^2 + 6$

4. At Chez Antoine Restaurant, the cashier takes in 138 pennies a day, beginning with his opening on July 1. On what day will he take in the 5,000th penny?

5. a. Measure the chocolate-covered beetle in inches. (Round to the nearest half-inch.)

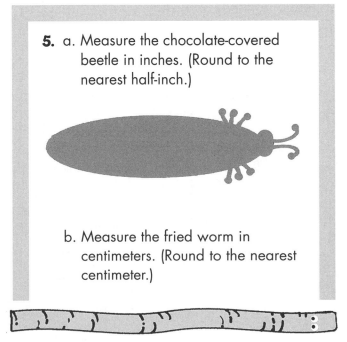

b. Measure the fried worm in centimeters. (Round to the nearest centimeter.)

1. Is the computation correct?

$$\begin{array}{r} \$\ 66{,}503.29 \\ -\ \ 18{,}266.54 \\ \hline \$\ 58{,}347.75 \end{array}$$

3. Estimate the answer:

$$(9{,}893 + 2{,}121) - 3{,}006 =$$

2. Which measurements are reasonable?

    a. A little girl drinks a 10 L milkshake.

    b. A restaurant serves hamburgers weighing 3.5 grams each.

    c. The entrance to a café is 3 meters high.

    d. A coffee shop serves their coffee in cups that hold ten ounces.

4. If b = –2, what is a?

$$12 - 3b^2 + a = 40$$

    a. 16

    b. –16

    c. 40

    d. –40

5. Challenge Problem

Kate and Nate meet for lunch at their favorite bistro. They love the unusual food! The restaurant adds a six percent state tax to all orders.

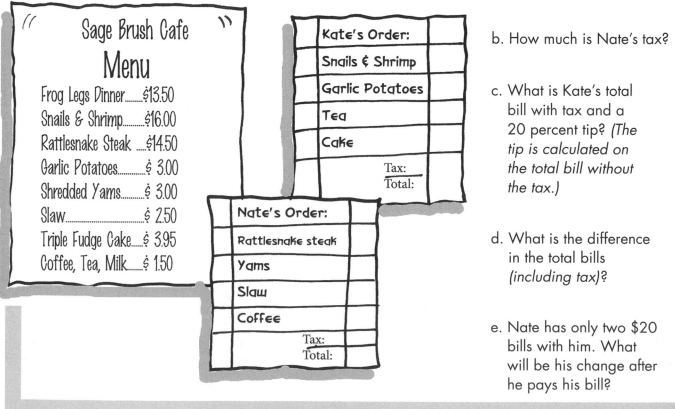

Sage Brush Cafe
Menu

Frog Legs Dinner......... $13.50
Snails & Shrimp........... $16.00
Rattlesnake Steak $14.50
Garlic Potatoes........... $ 3.00
Shredded Yams........... $ 3.00
Slaw.............................. $ 2.50
Triple Fudge Cake..... $ 3.95
Coffee, Tea, Milk....... $ 1.50

Kate's Order:
Snails & Shrimp
Garlic Potatoes
Tea
Cake
Tax:
Total:

Nate's Order:
Rattlesnake steak
Yams
Slaw
Coffee
Tax:
Total:

a. How much is Kate's tax?

b. How much is Nate's tax?

c. What is Kate's total bill with tax and a 20 percent tip? *(The tip is calculated on the total bill without the tax.)*

d. What is the difference in the total bills *(including tax)*?

e. Nate has only two $20 bills with him. What will be his change after he pays his bill?

1. What information is missing that is needed to solve this problem?

> A toaster uses infrared radiation to heat a piece of bread. One 4-slice toaster has a timer set to cook the toast for 2.3 minutes. How long will it take to toast all the bread slices in one loaf?

Mmmm, cinammon toast.

2. Compute: $33 \overline{)1,489}$

3. Lucy goes to buy a smoke detector. The store has a total of 18. They are not aware that five of them are defective. She buys two. What is the probability that both will be in good working condition?

4. Find two number pairs (n, m) that will solve the equation:

4n = 3m

5. What geometric space figure does this cell phone most resemble?

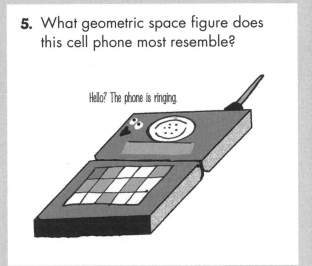

Hello? The phone is ringing.

1. A company that makes garage door openers ships 300 to a hardware store. The total load weighs 1,350 pounds. How many more openers would be needed for the shipment to total a ton?

2. Compute: **4,200 × (−1.4) =**

3. What is the LCM of 9 and 6?

4. Is this a correct graph of **x > −5**?

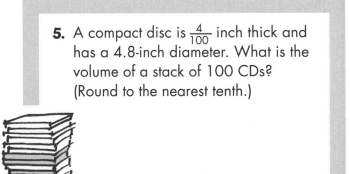

5. A compact disc is $\frac{4}{100}$ inch thick and has a 4.8-inch diameter. What is the volume of a stack of 100 CDs? (Round to the nearest tenth.)

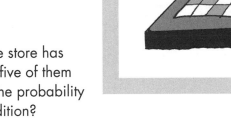

Quite a stack.

1. Compute: **–120 – 16 – (–20) =**

2. The electromagnet was invented in July, 1825. How many months have passed since then?

3. Simplify the expression.

$2n^2(6n^5 + 7)$

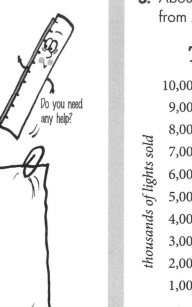

Do you need any help?

4. Draw an isosceles trapezoid.

5. About how much did sales increase from April to June?

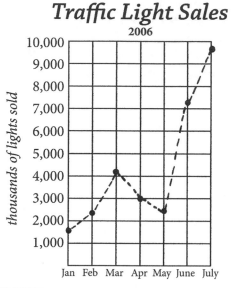

Traffic Light Sales
2006

thousands of lights sold

Jan Feb Mar Apr May June July

1. What is nine and eight-tenths divided by three and five-tenths?

2. An electric doorbell takes a 120-volt household current and steps it down to a 10-volt current, then passes this through an electromagnet. Write a ratio to compare the beginning current to the lower current.

3. True or false:

Any rational number can be written as the quotient of two integers.

4. Solve the equation.

$36 = 4n^2 - 5(n^2 - 9)$

5. Find the surface area of this smoke detector.

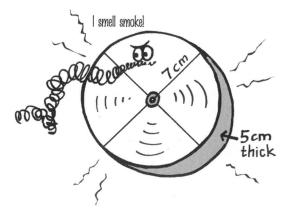

I smell smoke!

7 cm

5 cm thick

Name

1. Fill in the missing operation.

$$8{,}000 \;\boxed{}\; 250 = 32$$

4. In the equation y = 3x, if x = –5, what is y?

2. The number of radio frequencies each cell phone carrier gets to use in a city is a three-digit, even number. The sum of the digits is 13. The hundreds digit is four times the ones digit. What is the number?

3. Six friends each bought a digital camera. The prices they paid were:

$320.00 $216.00

$197.00 $245.00

$196.00 $410.00

What was the average cost of a camera?

I'm monitoring your answers.

---

5. Challenge Problem

This is the answer: **$6,925.00**

What is the problem?

A. Max's company bought new laptop computers. They paid $1,350 each for three computers and $250 each for service contracts. They bought software for $275. What did they spend all together?

B. A smoke detector may seem complicated with its photoelectric detectors and loud electric horn, but you can buy one for as little as $7.00. A school bought 725 at this price and sold them for a school fundraiser. They collected $12,000 for the sale of all the detectors. What was their profit?

C. A shipment of toasters was lost at sea. The container had 2,200 toasters valued at $6.50 each. The insurance covered 65 percent of the loss. How much was not covered?

D. An electronic keyboard that had been used to write a hit song sold for a high price at an auction. The price was $1,450 less than the amount paid at the same auction for an electric guitar. The total for both instruments was $8,425. What was the cost of the keyboard?

---

1. Compute: **6,000 x 444 =**

2. Describe the difference between independent events and dependent events in a probability experiment.

3. Is the number pair (20, 4) a solution to the equation below? *(x = 20 and y = 4)*

$$15 + 3y^2 = 2x - 7$$

4. Name this figure.

How many faces?

How many edges?

How many vertices?

I'm on my way to the 23rd century.

5. In the famous H.G. Wells novel, *Time Traveller*, a man is rocketed into the future by his time machine—stopping in the year 802,701.

   a. If Joe took a trip in that machine, leaving in 2006 and arriving in 802,701, how many years would he leap ahead?

   b. If Moe took a trip that rocketed ahead $\frac{2}{5}$ as far as Joe's, in what year would the machine stop?

   c. If Bo took a trip that rocketed ahead $\frac{6}{10}$ as far as Joe's, in what year would the machine stop?

1. Compute: **10.035 − 5.503 =**

2. Zelda found a time capsule on March 1, 2000. It had been buried on August 30, 1991. How many days had it been buried?

3. Simplify the expression.

6b − 7a − 12 + b + 9 + c − 3a

4. Round these to the nearest whole number.

   a. $2\frac{1}{5}$ c. $8\frac{6}{9}$

   b. $\frac{7}{12}$ d. $\frac{16}{3}$

The sands of time keep falling.

5. The students at Hendricks Middle School planned to build and sell decorative hourglasses to raise funds for their field trips. Each hourglass would contain four ounces of sand. Each grade (6th, 7th, 8th) had five homerooms, and each homeroom hoped to sell 250 hourglasses.

The third-period eighth-grade math class was asked to solve the problem of how much sand was needed. The students calculated that they should buy thirty 500-pound bags of sand for this project. Is this a reasonable solution?

1. True or false?

    a. Vertical angles are congruent.

    b. Two perpendicular, intersecting lines form four right angles.

2. Use words to write the expression.

$$9 + \frac{4x}{12}$$

3. When Professor Zoom gets into his time machine, he has no idea where he will travel in time. The machine can go to any of these years: 2050, 1862, 1630, 1815, 2210, 950, or 1444. What is the probability that Professor Zoom will travel to the nineteenth century?

4. Compute: $-330 \times 5(x - 13) =$

5. Describe the first operation you will do to solve this problem.

    Julia checked her sundial and found that the time was 9:35 a.m. The next time she checked, $6\frac{3}{4}$ hours had passed. What was the time on her second check of the dial?

My shadow tells me it's time for math class.

1. Compute: $\frac{13}{15} + \frac{7}{12} =$

2. What is the coefficient of p^3?

$$p + 3p^2 - 6p^3 + 12p$$

3. Round to the nearest ten thousand.

60,974,326

4. Which time capsule has the greater surface area?

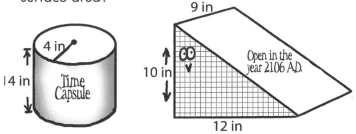

5. Write an equation that will help you solve the problem. Find the solution.

    Two scientists left in 2004 at the same time in their time machines for travel back into history. Professor Zoom's trip took him back 215 years farther than Professor Surch. The sum of the number of years they traveled was 563. To what year did Professor Zoom travel?

1. Estimate to decide which quotient is greater.

   a. $17\overline{)1,904}$ **b.** $3,256 \div 37 =$

2. Compute: **90,000,000 ÷ 4,500 =**

3. Solve the equation.

   $-666 - 12x^2 = -966$

   Could x also be the opposite number?

4. In all, 6,000 people showed up to watch the demonstration of Dr. Sylvester's time machine. The demonstration concluded with the launching of the machine. (It disappeared into thin air, leaving a trail of smoke.) As the audience left, they were surveyed to find out how many would want to take part in a time travel experiment. Of the first 100 surveys reviewed, 59 said they would take the chance. Based on this, how many people of the total crowd do you predict will say yes to time travel?

5. Challenge Problem

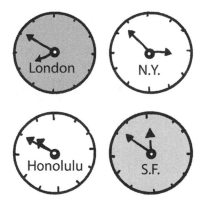

A. Ethan and Rosa each began a trip in Philadelphia, Pennsylvania (Eastern Standard Time) at 1:17 p.m. Ethan took a flight to San Francisco, California (Pacific Standard Time). The total flight time was five hours, 58 minutes. Rosa flew to Miami, Florida (Eastern Standard Time) and arrived at 4:02 p.m. How long was Rosa in Miami before Ethan arrived in San Francisco?

B. Chuck's grandfather clock chimes every 15 minutes: on the hour, half-hour, and quarter-hour. His own grandpa arrived at Chuck's home at 11:50 a.m. on Tuesday and left at 6:10 a.m. on Friday. How many times did the clock chime during Grandpa's visit?

No one knows how to program the time on this DVD player.

C. Bill is the timekeeper for a long marathon race, but Bill has a sticky problem. His watch loses six minutes every half-hour. His watch is correct when the race begins at 9:30 a.m. When the last runner comes in, Bill's watch registers a time of 2:15 p.m. What is the actual time?

1. Compute:

22,000 x 40,000 =

2. The Great Wall of China, one of the world's great wonders, is 23,560,000 feet long. Write this number in scientific notation.

3. What will determine whether the answer will be a positive or negative number?

$-b^3 + (-12) =$

4. What space figure is most like the Leaning Tower of Pisa?

Don't lean on me.

5. Leonardo has a chance to win a trip to see one of these wonders of the world. He will draw an envelope from a box that has one envelope for each of these places. What is the probability that he will draw tickets to see something that is outside North America?

Eiffel Tower

Niagara Falls

Ruins of Rome

Rock of Gibraltar

Grand Canyon

Great Pyramid

1. Simplify the equation.

$q + p + 8 = 2(q - 2)$

2. Write the fractions in lowest terms.

$\frac{8}{22}$ $\frac{5}{45}$ $\frac{12}{60}$

How far did Niagra fall?

3. In 1931, about 80,000 tons of rock fell from the American side of Niagara Falls. In 1954, about 185,000 tons broke off from the same area. How many pounds of rock is this?

4. Compute: **0.33 ÷ 0.6 =**

5. Set up a proportion and solve the problem. Show your work.

A large group of high school students set off on a climb to Machu Picchu. Nine out of the first group of 22 made it the whole way on the first day. At this rate, how many students out of the entire group of 176 will make it all the way to the top of the ruins?

1. Give the measure of each angle.

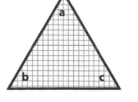

2. Compute:
   What is the difference between negative nine hundred fifty and twelve hundred?

3. Solve the equation.

   −11c = 4c − 70

4. A child in Paris let go of a new balloon. It rose to a height of 316.8 feet. This is 30 percent of the height of the Eiffel Tower. How tall is the tower?

   I can make it to the top of the Eiffel Tower.

5. The Panama Canal is one of the world's great feats of engineering. The 50-foot-long waterway took 34 years to complete. On the average, how many feet of the canal were completed each month?

   a. 6   d. 0.122
   b. 2.7   e. 17.6
   c. 8.16   f. 2.54

1. Compute: $\frac{5}{3} \times \frac{2}{6} \times \frac{1}{9} =$

2. After walking across the Golden Gate Bridge in San Francisco, California, Sam bought a copper replica of the structure. He paid for the $12.75 souvenir with a $50 bill. Describe three different possibilities for the change he received.

3. Solve the problem. Write the answer in scientific notation.

   $(18.06 \times 10^9) \div (4.3 \times 10^3) =$

4. What number is 1.0909 greater than 0.499?

What is the Chunnel?

5. What measurement unit would you use to find . . .

   a. the length of the Chunnel?

   b. the time that has elapsed since the Taj Majal was built?

   c. the weight of each block of stone used in the construction of the Great Pyramid?

   d. the amount of water that flows over Niagara Falls in an hour?

   e. the amount of water a hiker drinks on a day hike along the Great Wall of China?

   f. the height of the Space Needle?

Name

1. Which is greater?

    a. 30% of $1,400

    b. 18% of $2,000

    c. 65% of $975

    d. 9% of $3,950

2. Is this solution accurate?

$$95 - 8x = x^2 + (-114)$$
$$x = 11$$

3. The value of 3.052×10^7 is

    a. 305,200,000

    b. 35,200,000

    c. 30,520,000,000

    d. 30,520,000

4. Compute:

$$1,234 \times 5,000 =$$

5. Challenge Problem

The Japanese bullet trains are amazing feats of ingenuity and engineering. Thousands of people travel throughout Japan every day at speeds of up to 300 kilometers per hour. Great numbers of these commuters are occupied with an extremely popular number puzzle called Sudoku.

The puzzle contains nine blocks (or cells) of nine squares within a large square. This puzzle is solved by placing the digits 1– 9 one time each in each row and column. In addition to this rule, each of the digits may appear only once in each nine-space cell. Sudoku puzzles range in difficulty from fairly easy to very difficult. See how fast you can solve this easy Sudoku puzzle.

7		5		8		3		6
1	6		9		7		4	2
	4	8	3		6			5
4		6	7	2	3	9		8
5		9	1		8		6	
3			6	9	5	1	7	
9	3		8		4	5	2	1
		1		3		4	8	
	5	4	2		1		3	9

1. Compute:

$$\begin{array}{r} 22{,}489 \\ 87{,}654 \\ +\ \ 4{,}567 \\ \hline \end{array}$$

2. At Ashton School, all the lost gloves and mittens are gathered in a barrel. Today, there are 14 gloves and 20 mittens. Sue reaches in and grabs a mitten. She reaches in again. What is the probability that she will grab a mitten the second time?

3. Simplify the expression.

$$\frac{16n}{4} - 2n + 12$$

4. Which has more faces: a hexagonal prism or a pentagonal pyramid?

5. On February 20, 2001, Harvey Johnston's golden retriever, Max, disappeared. Harvey searched for months, and finally had to give up hope of finding Max. On August 13, 2005, Max showed up in the backyard, looking healthy and happy. Harvey has no idea where Max spent all that time, but he is delighted that the dog is no longer lost. How many days was Max lost?

1. Compute: $90.7 \times 9.07 =$

2. In February of 2006, a sick whale lost its way and swam up the Thames River into central London. Experts calculated that the whale was about 40 miles away from its home in the North Sea. How many kilometers is this?

3. Solve the equation.

$$10b + 6 - b = -3$$

4. An eighth-grade class has 184 students and 23 lost backpacks. Write a ratio that compares the number of students to the number of lost backpacks.

5. Find the volume of this container for lost socks.

Lost Sock Hopper

40 cm
35 cm
30 cm
10 cm

1. What is the mean of these temperatures?

19°   –4°   –22°   12°   50°   10°   –9°

2. Choose the name of a day at random. What are the odds in favor of getting a day that contains the letter **s**?

3. True or false?
A combination is a selection of a set of things from a larger set without regard to order.

4. A shipping company lost two cylinders. One had a radius of 30 cm and a height of 78 cm. The other had a height of 3.12 m and a radius of 1.2 m. Are these similar figures?

We made a break for freedom.

Sink your teeth into this problem.

5. Will the equation solve the problem?

A delivery company lost a package of false teeth that was on its way to a dental office. The package contained 14 sets of teeth. Each set had 28 teeth. Interestingly enough, the package had been dropped and had broken apart. Someone found a total of 116 teeth scattered about the sidewalk. What percentage of the original teeth were found?

$$\frac{116}{14} = \frac{28}{x}$$

1. Compute: $2\frac{5}{7} \times 10\frac{2}{3} =$

2. The measure of one angle in a trapezoid is 43°. The measure of of another angle is 88°. A third angle measures 100°. What is the measure of the fourth angle?

3. In the statement **10 – x ≥ –6**, which of these could be **x**?

15	**–6**	**0**
18	**20**	**–3**

4. Is this a correct statement?

$$\frac{7}{8} \approx \frac{49}{64}$$

We got lost at Disneyland.

And we hope nobody finds us.

5. Each year, the Lost and Found at Disneyland in California collects about a surprising number of objects. To find this number, follow the clues:

- an even, six-digit number
- no digits > 4
- five even digits
- last four digits the same
- highest place has odd digit
- digit in hundred thousands place < digit to its right
- sum of digits = 5

1. Finish the equation to demonstrate the **associative property**. (8 + 4k) + 66 =

2. At Marine World, Sasha lost her new digital camera when it fell 46 meters to the bottom of the porpoise tank. How many inches was this drop?

3. Write an equation to match the words.

The difference between ninety-eight and a number (b) equals thirteen times the number (b).

4. What is the area of the figure?

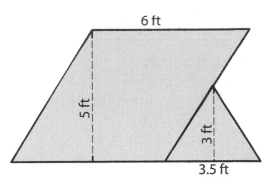

6 ft

5 ft

3 ft

3.5 ft

5. Challenge Problem

Here's what Stephanie and Sam did yesterday at Cosmic Park (in the order described). They arrived at the entrance at noon. They rode the Nebula Twirl, then visited the Starburst Arcade. Next, they rode the Big Dipper and the Rocket Plunge. They took a restroom break and ate an asteroid icicle. They rode the Saturn Slide and ate lunch at the Neutron Café. After another ride on the Big Dipper, they left through the same entrance at which they had arrived. How far did they walk inside the park? (Measure to the dots which show the entrance to each attraction.)

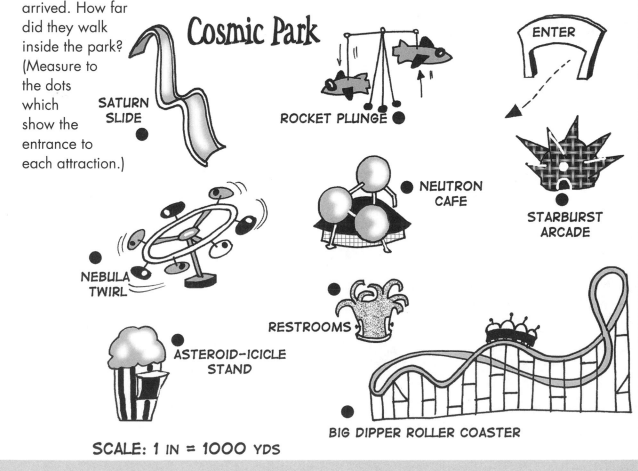

Cosmic Park

ENTER

SATURN SLIDE

ROCKET PLUNGE

NEUTRON CAFE

STARBURST ARCADE

NEBULA TWIRL

RESTROOMS

ASTEROID–ICICLE STAND

BIG DIPPER ROLLER COASTER

SCALE: 1 IN = 1000 YDS

1. Joey, the youngest member of the Better Late Than Never Band, is 204 months old. The oldest member, Maxine, is 1612 weeks older. How old is Maxine?

2. Compute:

$$68 \overline{)5{,}236}$$

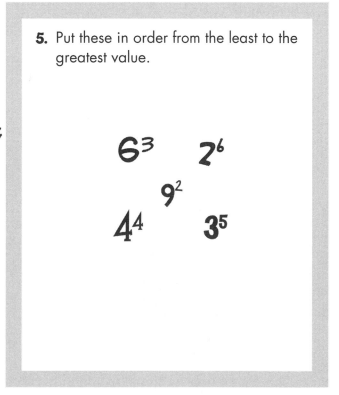

I make a good drumstick.

3. Someone picks a number between 80 and 115. What is the probability that it will be an odd number with three digits?

4. Describe the pattern. Fill in missing numbers.

1,170	1,160	1,140
_____	1,070	_____

5. Finish the drawings to make them symmetrical.

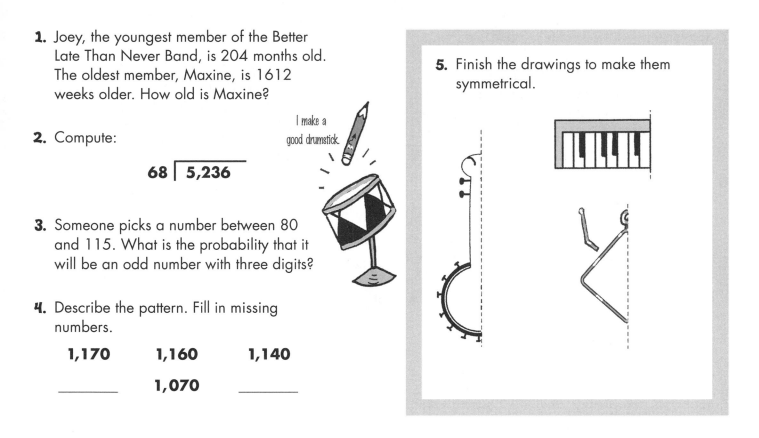

1. Subtract forty-three ten thousandths from one hundred sixty and twelve hundredths. Write the answer in standard notation.

2. How many like terms are in this expression?

$$5x + 9y^2 - y + 10x^3$$

That's noteworthy.

3. By 2004, the music group Black Eyed Peas had sold 529,400,000 copies of their album, *Elephunk*. If the average price received for a CD was $14.00, and 40 percent of the total went to the publisher, what is the amount of the publisher's earnings?

4. A drum has a 12 cm radius and a height of 40 cm. What is its surface area?

5. Put these in order from the least to the greatest value.

$$6^3 \quad 2^6$$
$$9^2$$
$$4^4 \quad 3^5$$

1. Compute: **123,456 – (–880) =**

2. Every year from 1990 – 2005, Fensworth High School hosted a concert by a local band. They have kept careful records of attendance and income from ticket sales. What would be the best way to display both parts of this data?

○ bar graph   ○ tally sheet

○ circle graph   ○ line graph

○ pictograph   ○ table

3. Solve the equation.

$$-3g = g + 96$$

Algebra makes my head spin.

4. Draw a rhombus with no right angles.

5. Estimate the solution to this problem.

A musical group called The String Cheese Incident inadvertently started a craze that revived the popularity of the hula hoop. They tossed hoops into the crowd at a concert so fans could start dancing. Now fans bring hoops to concerts and other celebrations. Manufacturers are selling fancy hoops for $38 per hoop. If 4,152 fans at a concert each buy a hoop at this price, how much has been spent?

1. Compute: $5\frac{1}{4} + \frac{2}{3} - \frac{5}{6} =$

2. The band Green Day had a major hit with their album *Dookie*. The album sold 19,000,000 copies globally. The American sales were 8,000,000. What percentage of the total sales were the American sales?

3. What are the place values of the 5's in this number?

25,054.655

4. Which operation should be done first?

7 – n(10 – 3) = –7

With those kinds of sales, they should change their name to "Green Bucks."

5. Could the total of the measures of all the central angles on the face of this tambourine be 180°?

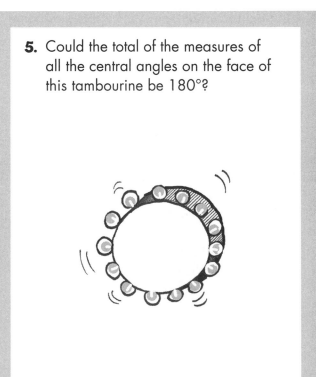

1. Find the average length of these songs on an album.

4.4 min	**6.2 min**	**1.9 min**
3.6 min	**2.7 min**	**2.2 min**

2. Which is the best estimate for the answer?

$8.3 \times \frac{1}{4} \times 205 =$

a. 6,400   d. 40

b. 600   e. 400

c. 4,000   f. 60

3. At an auction in 1998, a buyer paid $400,000 for Bernie Taupin's handwritten lyrics for "A Candle in the Wind." In 2003, a buyer paid $455,000 for John Lennon's handwritten lyrics for "Nowhere Man." Write a ratio (in lowest terms) comparing the cost of the Taupin song to the Lennon song.

4. Is this equation simplified correctly?

Equation: $5(4d^2 + 10) = 2,050$

Simplified: $d^2 = 100$

5. Challenge Problem

The Cliff Top Arena is under construction as a new concert venue. Your help is needed with the design. The arena needs 8,500 seats. Design a reasonable seating plan, showing how many seats could be in each of the sections in order to fit them all in. For each section, give the number of rows and the total number of seats. (You do not have to draw the seats!)

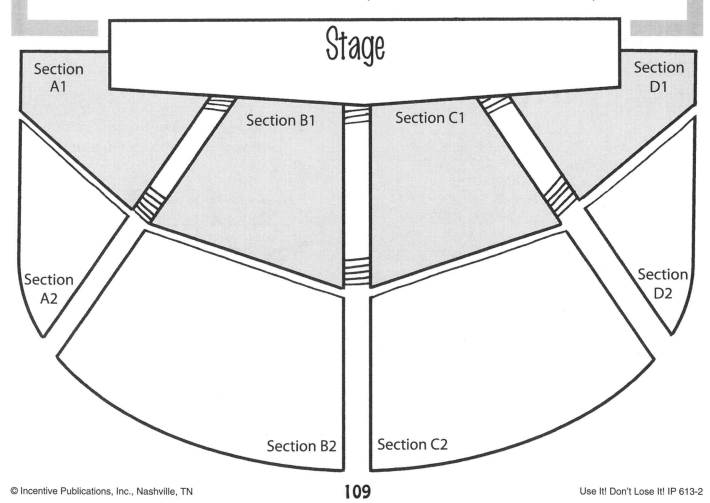

Name

1. In about 350 B.C., Greek thinker Plato wrote the story of Atlantis. The island kingdom supposedly existed about 900 years before Plato's time and flourished until it sank into the sea. Estimate the year it disappeared.

2. Compute:

$$12{,}345 \times 67$$

3. A surf shop is giving out decals with pictures of ancient Greek gods. Twenty decals picture Poseidon, eight decals picture Zeus, and seven picture Neptune. Chad is given a decal. What is the probability that it will picture Zeus?

4. Draw a space figure that has five faces.

5. Which pairs of numbers below (x, y) could be solutions to this equation?

$$-x = 2y + 4$$

a. (12, –4)
b. (12, –8)
c. (–10, –3)
d. (0, –2)
e. (6, 1)
f. (8, 6)

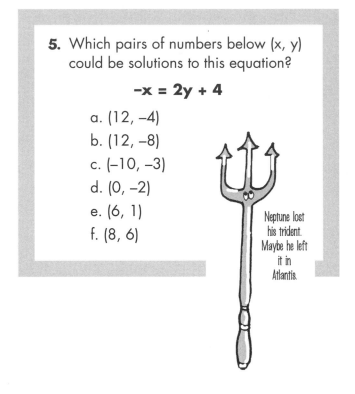

Neptune lost his trident. Maybe he left it in Atlantis.

Name

1. Compute: $12.5 \div 0.06 =$

2. Out of 216 passengers on a boat that is searching for Atlantis, 27 are children. At this rate, how many boat trips would it take to include 135 children?

3. If c = –6, what is d?

$$4d^2 - (-6) = 106$$

4. Some scholars believe that Atlantis was really the island of Thira in the Aegean Sea—an island which was destroyed by volcanic eruptions. It was 700 miles north of the island of Crete. Estimate this distance in kilometers.

5. Estimate the area of Neptune's crown. Give your answer in square units.

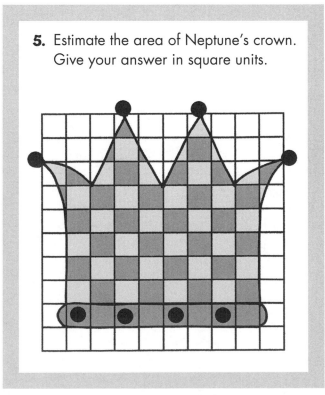

WEDNESDAY WEEK 36 _____ MATH PRACTICE
Name

1. Compute: **(–50 x –60) – (80 x 400) =**

2. There are 16 boxes, and each holds one gold replica of a mermaid or merman. Nine boxes contain mermaids. The rest hold mermen. Will is given one box. What are his odds against getting a merman?

a. $\frac{7}{16}$ c. $\frac{7}{9}$ e. $\frac{16}{7}$

b. $\frac{9}{16}$ d. $\frac{9}{7}$ f. $\frac{16}{9}$

3. Simplify the expression.

9f – 2g + 3(f + g) – 10f

4. Name all angles that are adjacent to angle ABD.

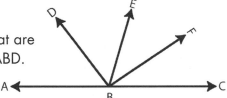

5. What information in the problem is not necessary for finding the solution?

Todd and Tara took a survey of 200 tourists after they had visited the Atlantis Resort in the Bahamas. Some 45 percent of those interviewed were children and 67 of those interviewed claimed that they believe Atlantis really existed. How many adults were interviewed?

Atlantis, Fact or Myth?

It could be true.

THURSDAY WEEK 36 _____ MATH PRACTICE
Name

1. 272 is what percent of 320?

2. Compute: $5\frac{2}{3} \times 3\frac{1}{6} =$

3. What is the coefficient of **n^2**?

$6m – n(5 + 12) – 4n^2 + 2n^3$

4. Alana searched for references to Atlantis. In 15 hours of searching, she found 330 literary references, articles, and websites. At this rate, how many did she find in six hours?

I've visited Atlantis on the web.

5. Convert these measurements.

a. 179 mm = _____ m

b. _____ mL = 20 L

c. 5 km = _____ mm

d. _____ cm = 0.4 m

e. _____ m^3 = 10,000 cm^3

f. 8,800 g = _____ kg

1. Fill in the missing operations.

$$-76 \,\square\, -40 \,\square\, 95 = -21$$

2. Sylvester Swum, a believer in the Atlantis story, searched in the Aegean Sea once every five years. He searched 12 days in 1980, 26 days in 1985, 36 days in 1990, 14 days in 1995, 27 days in 2000, and 29 days in 2005. What was the average number of days he searched per year?

3. Compute: **720,000 ÷ ___ = 9,000**

- ○ 90
- ○ 800
- ○ 80
- ○ 900
- ○ 8000
- ○ 80,000

4. Write the expression that matches the words.

negative forty less than nine times a number (n)

5. Challenge Problem

Plot the points at the locations shown below and connect them in order to show a picture of something you might expect to see if you visited the sunken kingdom of Atlantis.

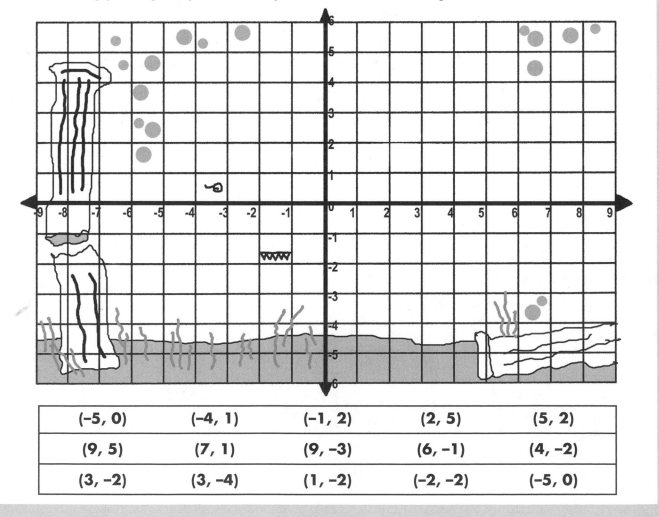

(–5, 0)	(–4, 1)	(–1, 2)	(2, 5)	(5, 2)
(9, 5)	(7, 1)	(9, –3)	(6, –1)	(4, –2)
(3, –2)	(3, –4)	(1, –2)	(–2, –2)	(–5, 0)

INCENTIVE PUBLICATIONS DAILY PRACTICE SERIES
GRADE 7 MATH SKILLS

Number Concepts

Skill	1	2	3	4	5	6	7	8	9	10	11	12	13	14	15	16	17	18	19	20	21	22	23	24	25	26	27	28	29	30	31	32	33	34	35	36
Numbers & Systems	✓	✓	✓																	✓	✓	✓		✓	✓	✓	✓		✓	✓	✓	✓	✓	✓	✓	
Whole numbers: read, write, compare, order	✓		✓	✓	✓	✓	✓	✓	✓	✓	✓	✓	✓	✓	✓	✓	✓	✓	✓	✓	✓	✓	✓	✓	✓	✓	✓	✓	✓	✓	✓	✓	✓	✓		✓
Whole numbers: place value	✓			✓	✓		✓																	✓					✓						✓	
Whole numbers: rounding	✓	✓											✓	✓						✓												✓				
Multiples, CM, LCM			✓																												✓	✓				
Factors, CF, GCF			✓	✓					✓															✓												
Divisibility				✓											✓									✓												
Exponential numbers; scientific notation		✓		✓				✓			✓	✓		✓	✓			✓	✓		✓	✓	✓					✓		✓			✓		✓	
Roots and radicals									✓		✓	✓		✓														✓									
Fractions: read, write, compare, order	✓	✓	✓	✓	✓	✓	✓	✓	✓	✓	✓	✓	✓	✓	✓	✓	✓	✓	✓	✓	✓	✓	✓	✓	✓	✓	✓	✓	✓	✓	✓	✓	✓	✓	✓	✓
Fractions: rounding								✓								✓							✓			✓					✓					
Equivalent fractions								✓		✓	✓	✓			✓	✓	✓									✓							✓			
Fractions in lowest terms					✓				✓	✓	✓					✓																				
Ratios						✓			✓	✓	✓		✓			✓	✓	✓	✓			✓	✓	✓	✓		✓			✓	✓	✓	✓	✓	✓	✓
Proportions			✓						✓	✓	✓	✓	✓			✓	✓	✓	✓							✓		✓		✓			✓			
Decimals: read, write, compare, order	✓	✓	✓	✓	✓	✓	✓	✓	✓	✓	✓	✓	✓	✓	✓	✓	✓	✓	✓	✓	✓	✓	✓	✓	✓	✓	✓		✓	✓	✓	✓	✓	✓	✓	✓
Decimals: rounding												✓															✓									
Percent	✓		✓		✓			✓		✓	✓	✓		✓									✓						✓	✓	✓	✓	✓	✓		✓
Fractions, decimals, percent relationships						✓							✓						✓										✓	✓						
Money			✓		✓		✓			✓	✓							✓	✓	✓	✓	✓		✓	✓		✓	✓	✓	✓	✓				✓	

113

© Incentive Publications, Inc., Nashville, TN

INCENTIVE PUBLICATIONS DAILY PRACTICE SERIES
GRADE 7 MATH SKILLS

Operations/Computations

Skill	1	2	3	4	5	6	7	8	9	10	11	12	13	14	15	16	17	18	19	20	21	22	23	24	25	26	27	28	29	30	31	32	33	34	35	36
Inverse operations							√										√													√						
Properties		√															√					√				√								√		
Order of operations			√	√				√					√	√			√	√				√		√					√						√	
Add and subtract whole numbers	√	√	√				√	√	√				√	√		√		√		√	√				√		√	√	√			√				√
Multiply whole numbers	√	√	√		√	√	√		√				√			√			√						√		√	√				√	√	√		√
Divide whole numbers			√		√	√	√		√		√		√					√	√			√			√		√					√	√			√
Multiply and divide with multiples of 10				√					√					√		√		√							√							√				√
Averages	√	√												√				√	√				√				√		√			√			√	√
Add and subtract fractions	√	√				√	√	√			√					√	√		√	√		√		√		√			√			√				
Multiply fractions		√			√				√		√		√		√	√		√		√				√	√		√				√			√		√
Divide fractions			√						√	√					√	√		√				√					√	√						√		
Add and subtract decimals	√	√	√			√	√		√		√		√			√				√			√		√			√	√		√	√	√			√
Multiply decimals		√			√						√											√			√		√	√				√				
Divide decimals			√	√	√	√	√				√		√	√			√	√	√	√		√				√							√			
Operations with money		√	√	√	√		√		√	√	√		√	√	√			√		√		√		√	√		√		√		√	√				√
Add integers	√				√	√		√			√				√	√		√						√	√			√	√					√		√
Subtract integers	√	√	√	√	√				√		√		√			√			√	√				√	√				√						√	√
Multiply integers											√		√		√					√		√	√	√	√						√			√		√
Divide integers			√				√		√		√		√		√			√	√			√					√						√			
Compute with roots, radicals, or exponents		√	√	√	√			√	√		√		√					√	√	√		√	√			√	√	√	√		√			√	√	√
Estimate answers	√	√	√		√	√	√	√	√		√		√	√			√							√	√	√			√	√		√		√	√	√
Find missing operation			√				√	√	√		√		√										√						√	√	√		√			√
Verify accuracy of computations				√	√		√	√	√		√						√			√		√		√	√	√			√	√		√				√

114

Use It! Don't Lose It! IP 613-2

INCENTIVE PUBLICATIONS DAILY PRACTICE SERIES
GRADE 7 MATH SKILLS

Problem Solving

Skill	1	2	3	4	5	6	7	8	9	10	11	12	13	14	15	16	17	18	19	20	21	22	23	24	25	26	27	28	29	30	31	32	33	34	35	36
Identify problem	√								√																											
Necessary information		√				√								√			√														√					√
Necessary operations; order of operations	√			√																	√		√													
Choose or explain strategy			√					√								√											√	√				√				
Translate into an equation			√		√		√						√					√		√		√				√						√		√		
Extend a pattern	√				√													√	√					√						√					√	
Use a formula		√		√		√		√	√		√	√		√				√				√		√					√			√			√	
Use diagrams/illustrations		√				√			√	√	√		√	√				√				√					√		√			√			√	
Use estimation		√					√		√				√				√			√	√				√				√	√				√	√	√
Use mental math	√		√						√		√								√		√			√	√					√						
Use logic					√									√	√						√			√									√			
Use trial and error				√							√			√	√		√							√		√	√				√	√				
Use a graph or table	√		√		√	√	√	√	√		√			√	√		√		√	√	√	√	√		√		√		√	√	√			√	√	√
Set up a proportion							√									√						√				√		√								√
Problems w/ whole numbers	√	√	√	√	√	√	√	√	√	√	√	√	√	√	√	√	√	√	√	√	√	√	√	√	√	√	√	√	√	√	√	√		√	√	√
Problems w/ fractions											√	√	√	√	√				√			√				√	√					√				
Problems w/ decimals		√		√	√	√		√		√	√	√	√	√	√	√		√	√	√	√	√	√	√			√		√	√	√					
Problems w/ percent		√	√	√	√	√				√	√	√	√				√		√		√	√		√				√		√			√		√	√
Problems with roots, radicals, or exponents									√											√		√					√						√		√	√
Problems w/ rate or ratio	√						√			√			√	√	√	√	√	√	√	√		√	√	√	√	√			√	√	√		√	√	√	√
Problems w/ money				√	√	√	√			√	√			√	√	√		√	√	√	√	√	√	√	√	√	√		√	√	√	√			√	√
Problems w/ time		√	√	√				√	√			√		√	√				√	√	√	√		√	√				√	√				√	√	√
Problems w/ measurement	√	√	√	√	√	√	√	√	√	√		√		√	√	√	√	√	√	√	√	√	√	√	√	√	√	√	√	√	√	√	√	√	√	√
Problems w/statistics	√	√	√	√	√	√	√	√	√					√	√	√	√	√	√	√	√				√		√		√	√	√	√	√	√	√	√
Problems w/probability		√					√	√			√		√						√										√		√	√		√		
Open-ended problems					√		√																	√												
Reasonableness or accuracy of solutions			√			√		√						√	√	√			√					√	√	√	√	√	√		√	√	√	√		

115

© Incentive Publications, Inc., Nashville, TN

Use It! Don't Lose It! IP 613-2

INCENTIVE PUBLICATIONS DAILY PRACTICE SERIES
GRADE 7 MATH SKILLS

Geometry

Skill	1	2	3	4	5	6	7	8	9	10	11	12	13	14	15	16	17	18	19	20	21	22	23	24	25	26	27	28	29	30	31	32	33	34	35	36
Points, lines, line segments, rays, and planes	√																															√				
Angles		√	√	√		√	√	√			√	√	√		√	√	√	√		√	√	√	√		√	√	√	√		√			√	√		√
Identify plane figures				√	√	√	√	√	√							√	√	√				√	√			√	√	√						√	√	
Properties of plane figures			√	√	√	√	√				√						√	√		√		√	√			√	√			√			√		√	√
Symmetry			√												√		√								√											
Transformations				√					√	√						√	√									√			√				√			
Identify space figures					√	√		√	√		√	√										√	√	√						√	√	√			√	
Properties of space figures					√	√		√	√		√			√						√		√		√	√			√			√			√		√
Similar figures					√								√		√									√	√											
Congruent figures						√				√	√									√									√							
Draw figures						√			√				√		√					√							√		√						√	√

Measurement

Skill	1	2	3	4	5	6	7	8	9	10	11	12	13	14	15	16	17	18	19	20	21	22	23	24	25	26	27	28	29	30	31	32	33	34	35	36
Measurement units	√	√	√	√		√	√		√											√						√						√	√	√		√
Estimate measurements				√			√														√			√	√			√								√
Convert units			√	√		√	√		√	√			√			√	√	√			√	√							√	√				√		√
Angle measurements	√	√			√		√			√						√	√			√		√		√	√	√				√		√		√		
Measure length	√						√		√			√					√										√			√						
Choose correct formula	√	√			√			√	√	√	√			√			√			√			√					√			√	√		√		√
Perimeter, circumference		√		√	√				√					√		√				√											√					
Area of plane figures				√	√		√		√				√	√				√	√	√	√	√		√	√								√	√		
Surface area (space figures)								√														√						√							√	
Volume of space figures		√							√	√	√				√	√	√		√	√	√	√		√		√			√	√				√		√
Temperature						√			√								√		√			√									√		√			
Time		√						√							√							√		√		√			√				√	√		
Weight					√																				√	√	√									
Scale √																		√				√					√			√						
Reasonableness of a measurement																						√								√						
Compare measurements				√		√				√			√		√					√	√											√				

© Incentive Publications, Inc., Nashville, TN

Use It! Don't Lose It! IP 613-2

INCENTIVE PUBLICATIONS DAILY PRACTICE SERIES
GRADE 7 MATH SKILLS

Statistics & Graphing

Skill	1	2	3	4	5	6	7	8	9	10	11	12	13	14	15	16	17	18	19	20	21	22	23	24	25	26	27	28	29	30	31	32	33	34	35	36
Define statistical terms	√	√				√								√												√	√									
Interpret tables	√				√	√		√	√						√			√				√		√	√	√			√	√						
Find mean, range, median, mode in a set of data		√							√	√						√								√			√			√x						
Select appropriate graph			√								√	√					√					√						√							√	
Interpret graphs		√	√		√				√			√							√			√	√													
Solve problems from data	√	√	√	√	√	√	√	√	√	√			√	√	√			√	√		√	√	√	√		√			√	√	√	√	√		√	
Translate data into a graph or table								√	√	√											√		√													
Coordinate graphs							√			√						√				√	√			√					√							√

Probability

Skill	1	2	3	4	5	6	7	8	9	10	11	12	13	14	15	16	17	18	19	20	21	22	23	24	25	26	27	28	29	30	31	32	33	34	35	36
Define probability terms				√																																
Describe likelihood of an event			√	√		√								√	√					√												√				√
Outcomes of one event			√	√										√	√											√			√							
Probability of one event			√	√			√	√	√			√															√		√				√		√	√
Outcomes of two independent events					√	√										√							√							√						
Tree diagrams					√	√																√								√						
Probability of two independent events					√												√		√	√		√														
Outcomes/probability of two dependent events										√	√					√		√			√			√	√				√		√			√		
Combinations and permutations										√	√										√				√		√							√		
Odds for or against							√				√		√															√						√		√
Random sampling										√			√																√			√				

117

Use It! Don't Lose It! IP 613-2

© Incentive Publications, Inc., Nashville, TN

INCENTIVE PUBLICATIONS DAILY PRACTICE SERIES
GRADE 7 MATH SKILLS

Pre-Algebra

Skill	1	2	3	4	5	6	7	8	9	10	11	12	13	14	15	16	17	18	19	20	21	22	23	24	25	26	27	28	29	30	31	32	33	34	35	36
Identify characteristics of different numbers	✓																												✓							
Patterns and functions		✓	✓		✓	✓	✓		✓			✓						✓		✓	✓	✓	✓	✓		✓	✓		✓	✓		✓		✓	✓	✓
Opposites; absolute value	✓			✓			✓									✓						✓						✓								
Compute with positive and negative numbers	✓	✓	✓	✓	✓	✓	✓	✓	✓	✓	✓	✓	✓	✓	✓	✓	✓	✓	✓	✓	✓	✓	✓	✓	✓	✓	✓	✓	✓	✓	✓	✓	✓	✓	✓	✓
Identify terms, variables, and coefficients		✓		✓		✓			✓					✓									✓													
Read and write expressions	✓	✓	✓	✓	✓	✓					✓	✓	✓		✓	✓	✓	✓			✓			✓	✓					✓	✓	✓			✓	✓
Simplify expressions		✓		✓	✓	✓		✓			✓	✓	✓			✓	✓	✓					✓							✓	✓	✓		✓		
Read, write, graph inequalities						✓	✓				✓		✓	✓	✓			✓	✓								✓				✓					
Read and graph points on a coordinate grid							✓						✓		✓						✓					✓										
Read and write equations			✓			✓	✓	✓	✓	✓	✓	✓	✓	✓	✓	✓	✓	✓	✓	✓	✓	✓	✓	✓	✓	✓	✓	✓	✓	✓	✓	✓	✓	✓	✓	✓
Match equations to problems				✓	✓											✓		✓				✓			✓	✓						✓		✓		
Simplify equations		✓					✓						✓	✓		✓					✓		✓			✓	✓		✓				✓		✓	
Solve equations – one variable, one step		✓											✓						✓		✓						✓									
Solve equations – one variable, multiple steps							✓	✓	✓		✓				✓		✓		✓	✓		✓		✓		✓		✓			✓	✓		✓		
Solve equations with two variables						✓			✓	✓	✓				✓					✓	✓	✓		✓	✓		✓		✓	✓	✓	✓			✓	✓
Order of operations in equations				✓					✓	✓								✓				✓						✓	✓		✓	✓				
Verify accuracy of solutions								✓				✓			✓					✓			✓							✓	✓				✓	

118

© Incentive Publications, Inc. Nashville, TN   Use It! Don't Lose It! IP 613-2

Week 1 (pages 5–7)

MONDAY
1. 1,161
2. Rule: Double the number and add 1;
   double the number and add 2;
   double the number and add 3;
   and so on . . .;
   next three numbers: 184, 375, 758
3. mean
4. Check drawings to see that lines are perpendicular.
5. no

TUESDAY
1. b,d
2. 66,066
3. 4.96
4. grams, liters, kilometers, meters
5. The length and width of the footprints.

WEDNESDAY
1. multiplication
2. acute
3. 37
4. –8
5. June, July, August

THURSDAY
1. | 135 |
2. $^7/_8$
3. 22; 202; 220; 2,022; 2,202; 20,200
4. 13,620
5. a. 8 cm; b. 16 in

FRIDAY
1. –36
2. 9315
3. b
4. c
5. a. Hugh; b. Lou; c. Bigfoot prints

Week 2 (pages 8–10)

MONDAY
1. Estimates will vary. 9,000–10,000 feet
2. a
3. 16,665
4. Jan, Feb, Mar, Apr, May, Jun, Jul, Aug, Sep, Oct, Nov, Dec
5. a, b, d, f

TUESDAY
1. six hundred thousand
2. 3
3. 1.56
4. meters
5. multiplication and division

WEDNESDAY
1. 18,009

2. triangle or isosceles triangle
3. b
4. –60
5. about 70%

THURSDAY
1. 0
2. $^1/_3$
3. 300 square feet
4. 37,410
5. c

FRIDAY
1. $^1/_3$
2. d
3. 100
4. 12 ft
5. A. 8 mi – 45 min
   B. 19 mi – 1 hr, 30 min
   C. 16 mi – 1 hr, 20 min
   Total time – about $3\frac{1}{2}$ hours

Week 3 (pages 11–13)

MONDAY
1. 2,176 ÷ 32 = 68 OR
   2,176 ÷ 68 = 32
2. b
3. 10x + 5
4. April, June, September, November
5. a. about 60 oz;
   b. about 6 oz a minute

TUESDAY
1. 15.82
2. 3, 19, 29, 31
3. –18
4. A, C, D
5. Wade

WEDNESDAY
1. a
2. no
3. –5
4. a
5. two weights at the top, the circle

THURSDAY
1. a number (d) divided by ten
2. 122 kg
3. $^4/_9$
4. 28, 56, 84, 112
5. $^8/_{15} = ^{40}/_x$ (Answer is 75)

FRIDAY
1. 120
2. 80
3. 1, 3, 7
4. c
5. a. yes; b. no (57 kg); c. no (Maria);
   d. yes; e. yes; f. yes (Bernadette)

Week 4 (pages 14–16)

MONDAY
1. 12.65 mph
2. 126,000
3. c
4. c
5. Julia's

TUESDAY
1. 3.2
2. b
3. 8n and 2n, and 16 and 50
4. T
5. just over 27 hours

WEDNESDAY
1. –300
2. 9
3. 3x + x = 18,500. x (Jack) = 4,625
4. pyramid
5. $^3/_6$ or $^1/_2$

THURSDAY
1. 3
2. y – 2x
3. 625
4. $^2/_3 + ^5/_9$
5. circumference of the canon

FRIDAY
1. yes
2. Add the numbers inside the parentheses.
3. 12 + 15b
4. 144 in^2
5. March 11, 1816

Week 5 (pages 17–19)

MONDAY
1. b
2. 86
3. 31g + 23
4. trapezoid
5. diesel engine car

TUESDAY
1. 3 to 5 or $^3/_5$
2. $92.46
3. two hundred four thousand, three hundred ten
4. 452.16 in^2
5. 4s + 2(4s) = 71,500

WEDNESDAY
1. 1 Q, 8 D, 3 N or 3 Q, 9 N; or 4 Q, 3 N, 5P, or 12 D
2. five times a number (p) divided by two
3. There are 14 different outcomes possible: h,S; h,M; h,T; h,W; h,Th; h,F; h,S; t,S; t,M; t,T; tW; t,Th; t,F; t,S

Use It! Don't Lose It! IP 613-2

4. 40
5. C, F

THURSDAY
1. a, b, d
2. $1^{17}/_{18}$
3. c
4. Rule is: subtract 20, add 10;
   Next three numbers are 70, 50, 60
5. yes

FRIDAY
1. a. 6; b. 0; c. 2; d. 3
2. b
3. multiply
4. $x + (x - 250) = 2100$; Solution is 1,175 miles
5. Cars are in this order, from right to left (first place to fifth place): Van, Fran, Nan, Stan, Dan or Van, Fran, Nan, Dan, Stan

Week 6 (pages 20–22)
MONDAY
1. 6b
2. $6 + (-2) = 4$
3. 23
4. A line segment is a portion of a line, marked by two endpoints.
5. Outcomes: cherry, $50; cherry, $20; cherry, $10; lime, $50; lime, $20; lime, $10; grape, $50, grape, $20, grape, $10

TUESDAY
1. <
2. twenty-five hundredths, 25%, one-quarter; one-fourth, $^1/_4$
3. 13.5222
4. 198 m^2
5. She has 7 photos of a Venus flytrap plant and 10 photos of a sundew plant. She spent 3 months searching for a pitcher plant and finally took 5 photos.

WEDNESDAY
1. $6n^2 = 96$
2. −48
3. range
4. no
5. d

THURSDAY
1. four hundred million, four million, forty thousand, forty
2. $^{10}/_3$
3. $4^1/_9$
4. 100° C and 212° F
5. 2005

FRIDAY
1. Answers may vary somewhat; 150
2. dependent; The outcome of the second event is affected by the outcome of the first event.
3. 20
4. a. y = 14; b. y = −14
5. A. white three-leaf, black three-leaf, dandelion puff; black three-leaf, white three-leaf, upside down dandelion puff
   Next three: dandelion puff; black three-leaf, white three-leaf
   B. 1 eye, 1 ear, 1 lips; 2 eyes, 2 ears, 2 lips, 3 eyes, 3 ears
   Next three: 3 lips, 4 eyes, 4 ears

Week 7 (pages 23–25)
MONDAY
1. yes
2. a, c
3. 35x = 70
4. 966 ÷ 23 = 42 OR 966 ÷ 42 = 23
5. (3, 0); (5, 2); (4, 5); (2, 6); (−1, 7); (−3, 3); (−4, 6); (−5, 4); (0,2)

TUESDAY
1. 0.66, 1,066, 1.6, 6.006, 6.06
2. rational
3. 0.429
4. 2 cm
5. The pattern is: Add 6, Add 8, Add 10, Add 12, and so on. July: 120 total; Aug: 138 total; Sept: 158 total

WEDNESDAY
1. −280
2. 360°
3. k = 73
4. yes (Answer is 20° difference)
5. a. $P = ^2/_{10}$ or $^1/_5$
   b. $P = ^1/_2$
   c. $P = ^2/_7$

THURSDAY
1. $^2/_9$; $^1/_2$; $^3/_5$; $^2/_3$
2. 24
3. $1^1/_4$
4. 18 square units
5. yes (x = 5 hours)

FRIDAY
1. $516.76
2. no; odds against are $^{11}/_3$
3. −20.04
4. no (Correct answer is 1914)
5. Answers may vary. One answer is:
   Sam – 28; Sneakers – 20;
   Clarisse – 40; Elaina – 60

Week 8 (pages 26–28)
MONDAY
1. $^{14}/_{17}$
2. $11b^2 - 7b$
3. 179,933 km
4. 81°
5. 49,440,000

TUESDAY
1. 2
2. 37.5 ft^2
3. y = $^1/_5$
4. 47
5. Tuesday, 3:57 a.m.

WEDNESDAY
1. 72 to Mali; 18 to Rome; 150 to Ecuador; 210 to New Zealand
2. −42
3. <
4. Answers will vary (cereal box, book, CD case).
5. 129.8 mi^2

THURSDAY
1. $^1/_{40}$
2. yes
3. $^6/_9$; $^{18}/_{27}$; $^{22}/_{33}$
4. no (Correct answer is d = −1,800)
5. Answer: 15,644; Operations: add, subtract (in this order)

FRIDAY
1. b
2. distributive property
3. 5.75×10^7
4. 199.5
5. a. 13,202,270
   b. 43,490.4 mi^2
   c. 781,651,5 mi^2
   d. 8,790,827
   e. 3,066 (3,074.4 in a leap year)

Week 9 (pages 29–31)
MONDAY
1. w = −22
2. a. $^8/_{18}$ or $^4/_9$;   b. $^{17}/_{18}$
3. subtraction inside the parentheses
4. 2
5. Estimates may vary somewhat: about 31 minutes

TUESDAY
1. $^3/_5$; $^7/_{12}$; $^4/_5$
2. two
3. 5.003
4. 21,371.625 ft^2
5. yes, both parts

WEDNESDAY

1. b
2. yes
3. 845
4. 23
5. Trapezoids will vary. Check to see that both figures are trapezoids.

THURSDAY

1. 1, 3, 5; GCF = 15
2. divide
3. grams, ounces, pounds
4. $n = c^8$
5. He is doing less and less fighting or having less success over the 5-year period.

FRIDAY

1. about 14,000
2. b, c, d, e
3. 2,000
4. Check to see that steps are shown. Subtract 6 from both sides to get $13p = 780$; Divide each side by 13 to get $p = 60$.
5. Check bar graphs to see that data is properly transferred into the graph format.

Week 10 (pages 32–34)

MONDAY

1. 23,156
2. n = 80
3. 720
4. Check drawings.
5. mosquito (17 lb), fish (26.4 lb), spider (30 lb)

TUESDAY

1. 75 to 45 or $^5/_3$
2. 19.69
3. $V = \pi r^2 \times h$
4. d
5. $y = 2x + 1$; 13, 17

WEDNESDAY

1. There are 6 different combinations possible: cyclone & train; cyclone & cattle; cyclone & river; train & cattle; train & river; cattle & river
2. –2,530
3. true
4. $s^3 = 64$
5. 45 lb beef cubes; 44 lb wild turkey meat; 80 T (or 5 C) crushed garlic; 70 lb sliced potatoes; $66^2/_3$ C carrot chunks; 55 C diced onions; 60 T (or $3^3/_4$ C) crushed oregano; 100 qt (25 gal) beef broth

THURSDAY

1. find the value of the squared number (multiply 5 by itself)
2. $-14 - 12 - 25 = t$ (answer: –51°)
3. $^{18}/_{25}$
4. 21
5. 240 m^2

FRIDAY

1. 7.697
2. –40
3. $516.03
4. C and D
5. a. 20 days   c. 12 min   e. 1344
   b. 216 men   d. 15 mi

Week 11 (pages 35–37)

MONDAY

1. 12,228,800
2. 102
3. six
4. the difference between fifty and three times the cube of a number (n)
5. a. T; b. T; c. T; d. F. e. T

TUESDAY

1. no
2. 5
3. $b^2 = 16$
4. 70 in^3
5. Answers will vary. Check for sensibility.

WEDNESDAY

1. c
2. x = 72
3. $^5/_{11}$
4. hexagonal prism
5. a. 0.35
   b. 80%
   c. 0.14
   d. 15%

THURSDAY

1. x = 5
2. $2^1/_{10}$
3. 142.5 m
4. <
5. 54

FRIDAY

1. b
2. no
3. k = –2
4. Check graph to see that: food takes up about $^4/_9$ of the circle; litter takes up about $^3/_9$ (or $^1/_3$) of the circle; vet bills take up about $^1/_9$ of the circle; and the last ninth is split between toys and grooming.

5. cats and exotic pets

Week 12 (pages 38–40)

MONDAY

1. $^{16}/_{20}$ or $^4/_5$
2. 30 = 10x
3. bar graph
4. F
5. a. 46; b. 1.5

TUESDAY

1. Approx $11^1/_2$ hrs
2. 4,042
3. three times a number cubed is greater than one hundred
4. 20.09
5. 13,816 cm^3

WEDNESDAY

1. 386
2. $t = ^d/_r$ (Answer: 11:30 pm)
3. sphere
4. $^{15}/_{185}$
5. first – Jesse (black umbrella); second – Zack (green umbrella); third – Roz (red umbrella)

THURSDAY

1. 4
2. 27
3. $-42 + 7d$ (or $7d - 42$)
4. 1.5%
5. $x + 15x = 6,400$; $x = 400$

FRIDAY

1. multiply
2. –11
3. $^1/_4$
4. Missing numbers from top to bottom:
   y = 0; x = –2; y = 2; x = –3; x = 2; y = 6
5. a. 640
   b. 800
   c. 1,440

Week 13 (pages 41–43)

MONDAY

1. 100 k/hour and 0.05 k/hour
2. 47,520
3. $y = 76^4/_{11} = 76.36$
4. h, i
5. Brad

TUESDAY

1. yes
2. 220 ft
3. 30,330,030 – 30,330,003 – 30,303,333
4. 56 m
5. about 7,000 hours

ANSWER KEY

WEDNESDAY
1. $5k^6$
2. 35,000 cm (or 350 m)
3. –86,420
4. 240
5. AB and EF; AB and WX

THURSDAY
1. 300,000
2. $^9/_{12}$ or $^3/_4$
3. y = 6
4. 7,326.7 cm^3
5. yes

FRIDAY
1. yes
2. 80%; 0.8
3. associative for addition
4. 4,252 + 28,423 = 32,675
5. 8:30 am

Week 14 (pages 44–46)

MONDAY
1. 10,102
2. the number of times an item occurs in a set of data
3. 9 + 2x = 20
4. a plane figure base, five vertices, triangular faces in the number of sides of the base
5. Pyramids and Great Sphinx, Pyramid and Market, Great Sphinx and Market, Camel and Market, Great Sphinx and Camel

TUESDAY
1. $1,412.04
2. m = 19
3. 34.5 metric tons
4. 63,469,000
5. A = $^1/_2$bh

WEDNESDAY
1. –134
2. hexagonal pyramid or pentagonal prism
3. $^5/_{12}$
4. 22b
5. c

THURSDAY
1. 66m
2. 2$^1/_3$
3. 35,104,202
4. 654
5. trapezoid

FRIDAY
1. 280,000,000
2. d
3. a. 19; b. 31
4. division inside the parentheses

5. a. The distance the camel would travel (the width of the Sahara Desert)
   b. The date of the king's death
   c. The year the mummy-preparing process was developed
   d. The length of the Nile
   e. The height of the Eiffel Tower

Week 15 (pages 47–49)

MONDAY
1. 12,831
2. 212, R 21
3. 16
4. Check student drawings to see that figures are similar.
5. a. $^2/_8$ or $^1/_4$
   b. $^5/_8$
   c. $^5/_8$

TUESDAY
1. 3045 mi
2. 147,175
3. 11n = 66
4. 8.7
5. Order of operations may vary: Multiply (8 x 10); multiply (4 x 14); (80 + 56); (136 x 3); Answer is 408

WEDNESDAY
1. –51
2. 26$^1/_8$
3. 3, 4, 0, –1
4. Check student drawings to see that triangles are scalene (no equal sides or angles)
5. 74

THURSDAY
1. <
2. no
3. 28° C
4. $^{25}/_{66}$
5. 71%

FRIDAY
1. anywhere from 200,000 to 280,000
2. 5,760,000 or 5.76 x 10^6
3. n = 9
4. a. A and C
   b. B
   c. B and D
5. 10 triangles; 4 parallelograms; 6 trapezoids

Week 16 (pages 50–52)

MONDAY
1. 122,210
2. 2,700 m^2
3. 3p = 36
4. six: cy, cj, cs, yj, ys, js
5. triangle has 3 possible lines of

symmetry; hexagon has six possible lines of symmetry; necklace with diamond has one possible lines of symmetry; heart has one possible line of symmetry; square with cross has four possible lines of symmetry.

TUESDAY
1. 9
2. h = –14
3. 40$^1/_8$ mph
4. 12
5. buoy

WEDNESDAY
1. –89
2. the difference between ten and the cube of a number plus the square of the same number
3. 12 ft – 130 ft
4. a. rectangle; b. triangles;
   c. hexagon; d. squares;
   e. rhombus or parallelogram
5. Strategies will vary. Answer: 637

THURSDAY
1. a. 6$^6/_{11}$; b. $^5/_9$; c. $^4/_{55}$
2. 3.5 km
3. x = 6
4. $^{21}/_{16}$ or 1$^5/_{16}$
5. b

FRIDAY
1. yes
2. numbers that are the same distance from zero on opposites sides of zero on a number line
3. 60
4. $100, h; $100, t; $100, h; $100, t; $100, h; $100, t; $50, h; $50, t; $50, h; $50, t
5. a. cruise ship
   b. (–5, 4) (2, 2) (–3, –4) (5, –4)
   c. sailboat
   d. sailboat
   e. Check student grids to see that submarines are correctly placed.

Week 17 (pages 53–55)

MONDAY
1. 2
2. x = –55
3. 2,000
4. $^4/_{11}$
5. 20.4 mi

TUESDAY
1. 9.26 + 63.04 = 72.3
2. b = 9$^1/_3$
3. thousandths
4. 11,304 cm^3

5. Missing: the speed of the fastest human

WEDNESDAY
1. −9.2
2. circle graph
3. the product of a number (n) and the addition of another number (y) and negative three
4. 33 miles/hour
5. slide

THURSDAY
1. Add the numbers inside the parentheses.
2. $^{22}/_{55}$
3. $4\,^4/_5$
4. 68° F
5. 5%

FRIDAY
1. c
2. subtract
3. $8n^2 - 6n$
4. ten squared minus the sum of a number (p) and five
5. a. F; b. F; c. F; d. F; e. F; f. F

Week 18 (pages 56–58)

MONDAY
1. pentagon
2. 29q = 145
3. 334,299
4. $20,821.49
5. $28 – $84

TUESDAY
1. 300
2. no
3. no
4. 9 to 1 (or 9:1 or $^9/_1$)
5. yes

WEDNESDAY
1. $^2/_5$
2. 9,000
3. Answers will vary: Some possibilities: three 20's, three 5's, and two 1's, OR five 5's, one 50, and two 1's
4. ABE
5. c

THURSDAY
1. b = $45 – $31 – $39 – $17; b = −$42
2. $^7/_{15}$
3. quart, milliliter, pint, liter
4. >
5. 2x = −y or −y = 2x; pairs to finish are: (−2, 4); (−1, 2); (0, 0); (1, −2); (2, −4); (3, −6)

FRIDAY
1. $6.40
2. a. 3,200,000; b. 55,500; c. 609,000
3. y = 6
4. add ($0.20 + $13.00)
5. a. total screens   c. 62,747
   b. $3.30   d. $10.39

Week 19 (pages 59–61)

MONDAY
1. 24
2. 860
3. 1,464,000
4. x = 3
5. a. pentagon; b. parallelogram; c. square; d. rectangle; e circle.

TUESDAY
1. a. mi, ft, yd, or m
   b. in^3, cm^3, ft^3, or m^3
   c. in^2, ft^2, cm^2, or m^2
   d. hrs, min
2. g = −7.04
3. $365.10
4. 365.10
5. 18

WEDNESDAY
1. 76
2. triangles, parallelogram
3. b = −15
4. no
5. All flight attendants except Mark worked more hours in February than in January.

THURSDAY
1. $7\,^{11}/_{125}$
2.
3. 1
4. Answers will vary depending on today's date.
5. 4,750 m^2

FRIDAY
1. t = 479
2. 181
3. −47
4. 1,231
5. Answers will vary. Examine student drawings to look for repeating patterns.

Week 20 (pages 62–64)

MONDAY
1. 0, −30, 66, −1,000
2. yes
3. 121,401

4. Drawings will vary; check to see that they are cylinders.
5. Explanations will vary. Answer: 6 to 34 or $^6/_{34}$ or $^3/_{17}$ (Note: Odds against something other than a diamond are the same as odds in favor of its being a diamond.)

TUESDAY
1. y = any value because the equation reduces to 32 = 32
2. 3 ft
3. 81.8181
4. Bria
5. 43,560 cm^3

WEDNESDAY
1. false
2. 995
3. Equations may vary.
   1998 − 50 + 4 = x (Answer: 1952)
4. 6
5. $^{56,000}/_{12} = {^x/_3}$; 12x = 168,000; x = 14,000

THURSDAY
1. 2, 4, 6, 8, 9, 10, 12, 14, 15, 16, 18, 20, 21, 22, 24
2. 18 to 43 or $^{18}/_{43}$
3. $5\,^1/_5$
4. yes
5. a. 69.08 ft
   b. 379.94 ft^2

FRIDAY
1. 0.2
2. m = 30
3. $^4/_{35}$
4. b
5. a. 871   e. CMLXXVIII
   b. 1199   f. MCCCLXXVII
   c. 1925   g. MXVI
   d. 1837   h. MCMLXXII

Week 21 (pages 65–67)

MONDAY
1. 511,939,871
2. 20
3. nine times a number cubed minus twenty
4. a, d, e
5. 1249

TUESDAY
1. 10,962,500,000
2. $3y^2 + 5y = 68$
3. 222.902
4. the radius
5. a. 37   c. 92   e. 78
   b. 86   d. 99   f. 59

ANSWER KEY

WEDNESDAY
1. $40x + 50y^2$
2. part of a circle (or, the line segment that follows the outside edge of a circle between any two points on the edge of the circle)
3. 160,000
4. 240 oz
5. c, e, f, h

THURSDAY
1. Answers will vary depending on today's date.
2. $40\frac{19}{20}$
3. $b = -0.5$
4. 430,022
5. 1,054

FRIDAY
1. not correct: $2040 \times 20 = 40,800$
2. b, c, d
3. 72,000
4. Two events are independent if the occurrence of one event does not affect the probability of the occurrence of the other. These are independent events.
5. 2 jars red, 2 jars blue, 1 jar yellow, 7 jars black; total cost: $30.00

Week 22 (pages 68–70)

MONDAY
1. $116,000
2. 3,551
3. $120 - 5n = n$
4. a. 7   b. 15   c. 10
5. Estimates may vary slightly: tree-sitting: 10 hours; standing on head: 2 hours; sitting with snakes: 4 hours; standing on one leg: 5 hours; sitting on ice: 3 hours

TUESDAY
1. 12.5
2. $6,535$ in^3
3. $20,000 + 5000 + 600$
4. 39.5
5. c

WEDNESDAY
1. add 4b and 18b
2. about 378 calories
3. –55
4. b, c, f, e
5. Necktie is crossed out because it has no units; 4, 1, 6, 2, 5, 3

THURSDAY
1. 6^5
2. $d = 6$

3. $2\frac{2}{3}$
4. no
5. Examine tables to see that they are set up in a way that will help to solve the problem. (Answer is: $317,975.49)

FRIDAY
1. Answers will vary.
   (Example: $(6 \times 3) \times 5 = 6 \times (3 \times 5)$)
2. Answers will vary (Example: $(-6, 5)$)
3. 3,252,518
4. $\frac{4}{30}$ or $\frac{2}{15}$
5. A. no   C. yes   E. no
   B. no   D. yes   F. yes

Week 23 (pages 71–73)

MONDAY
1. $\frac{1}{1480}$
2. unlike
3. 21,184
4. hexagonal pyramid
5. Friday

TUESDAY
1. 37,019
2. 9.2140; 2.1409; 1.4092
3. 3.7158
4. 384 cm^2
5. b

WEDNESDAY
1. 3,000
2. six: 2 brown; brown & red; brown & black; 2 black; black & red; 2 red
3. $m - n = -12$
4. 248°
5. daddy-longlegs, grasshopper, house

THURSDAY
1. 380
2. Formula is: subtract 32, then multiply by $\frac{5}{9}$; Answer is 37.22°C
3. $-\frac{5}{20}$ or $-\frac{1}{4}$
4. $p = -50$
5. 225

FRIDAY
1. Strategies may vary. Convert each scientific notation number to standard notation, then subtract. Answer is: 2,864,000
2. 600
3. b
4. Correct answer is 1,933,074
5. Examine graphs and tally sheets for accuracy.

Week 24 (pages 74–76)

MONDAY
1. 2,880 k^2

2. $(596 + 42)$
3. $\frac{3}{13}$
4. c
5.

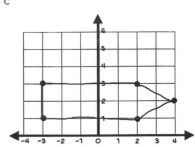

TUESDAY
1. one billions, one hundred millions, ten thousands, and hundreds
2. 48 lbs
3. $43.77
4. $x = 8$
5. a. $28\frac{1}{8}$
   b. $55

WEDNESDAY
1. 40
2. 8.44 kg
3. >
4. a, d
5. C, E, B, D, F, A

THURSDAY
1. $13k + 42$
2. six
3. 5
4. $52\frac{2}{15}$
5. a. $\pi r^2 h$
   b. c

FRIDAY
1. d
2. 730
3. $7d^2 + 19d = 66$
4. 122, 144
5. Max

Week 25 (pages 77–79)

MONDAY
1. 481,720
2. 9,000
3. $x - 4$
4. cube
5. 32 m

TUESDAY
1. Answers will vary. Check to see that all fractions are $< \frac{3}{7}$
2. 70.731
3. 344
4. 90m^2
5. b

WEDNESDAY
1. $^{11}/_{295}$
2. –79,000
3. 4.1 mi
4. 4
5. no; 4s + s + s = 12,000; d = 2,000

THURSDAY
1. $^1/_2$
2. $^8/_{15}$
3. Band-Aids
4. y = 15
5. October, 1923

FRIDAY
1. 2,160
2. 180
3. 97,300
4. b
5. 24: ZACS, ZASC, ZCAS, ZCSA,
   ZSAC, ZSCA, AZCS, AZSC,
   ACSZ, ACZS, ASCZ, ACSZ,
   CZAS, CZSA, CASZ, CAZS,
   CSZA, CSAZ, SZAC, SZCA,
   SACZ, SAZC, SCZA, SCAZ

Week 26 (pages 80–82)

MONDAY
1. 265 min or 4 hr, 25 min
2. 920
3. 10
4. Check student drawings to see that
   they have drawn the correct
   transformation (turn).
5. a

TUESDAY
1. 44 min
2. 3.5
3. x = 32
4. Answers will vary. Check to see
   that all fractions written are
   equivalent to $^6/_9$.
5. no

WEDNESDAY
1. 9
2. 19.23 lb
3. –6
4. 125°
5. flies

THURSDAY
1. $23^{11}/_{15}$
2. scale
3. thirty and two hundred three ten
   thousandths
4. (3, 13); (1, 3)
5. 1,800 mi

FRIDAY
1. a, d
2. 7x + 4 = 60
3. yes
4. d
5. 20

Week 27 (pages 83–85)

MONDAY
1. $^5/_{29}$
2. 40 = 8b
3. 10
4. Check drawings to see that the figures
   have five sides.
5. 42

TUESDAY
1. 1976
2. 17.60088
3. 100.0325
4. 12
5. 37.68 cm

WEDNESDAY
1. 16 years
2. –57
3. 10
4. m = $19^5/_9$
5. Check student line segments.

THURSDAY
1. 444 months
2. a. $^4/_5$ c. $^1/_3$
   b. $8^1/_2$ d. $2^2/_3$
3. $^{16}/_{27}$
4.
$$\xleftrightarrow{\quad\bullet\qquad\quad}$$
   -5 -4 -3 -2 -1 0 1 2 3 4 5
5. a. 57%   c. 43%   e. 27%
   b. 46%   d. 55%

FRIDAY
1. divide
2. 167
3. x = 5 (Explanations may vary.)
   Subtract 30 from both sides to get
   –15x = x – 80; Subtract x from both
   sides to get –16x = – 80; Divide both
   sides by –16 to get x = 5
4. a. Mode is the item that occurs most
      often in a set of data.
   b. 35
5. a. 15   c. 32,292   e. 2,300
   b. 1994   d. 25

Week 28 (pages 86–88)

MONDAY
1. 4,148,130
2. 64%
3. divide by –1, x = –42
4. $^6/_{44}$ or $^3/_{22}$

5. a. There are several choices:
      ADE, ADF, FDB, ADB, EDC
   b. There are several: DA, DF, DB, DC,
      DE
   c. BG
   d. line JK

TUESDAY
1. 1550%
2. 3.74×10^8
3. four times the difference between ten
   and a number (y) equals negative
   eight
4. $4276.68
5. 126 feet

WEDNESDAY
1. 9
2. –480
3. 35
4. 388
5. b

THURSDAY
1. y = 12
2. $^9/_{50}$; 0.18; 18%
3. $3^{13}/_{17}$
4. 130°
5. Problem-solving strategies will vary.
   Students will probably need to find
   the population of Rhode Island first,
   then Montana, then South Dakota,
   then Vermont. Answer: Vermont

FRIDAY
1. 2000
2. –x + 29
3. 1,362
4. a; Answer: 13.5 mi^2
5. a. 143,368,343
   b. 10,131,189
   c. 57.3%
   d. 41,077,577
   e. Answers will vary depending on
      the date.

Week 29 (pages 89–91)

MONDAY
1. 251.20 ft^2
2. Answers will vary depending on
   today's date.
3. 43,740,674
4.

5. 300

TUESDAY

ANSWER KEY

1. 379.953
2. $2x + (x + 10) = 37$
3. b
4. no
5. 2281 years

WEDNESDAY
1. Check to see that drawn figures are congruent.
2. 156
3. $y = 2$
4. –24,550
5.

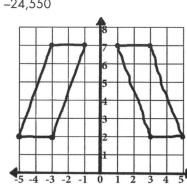

THURSDAY
1. 10:00
2. $6w = 30$
3. $10\,{}^{17}\!/_{45}$
4. $5,000
5. $5,355

FRIDAY
1. no (R is 4)
2. Divide both sides of the equation by 6.
3. 30 (19b)
4. c
5. a. ${}^1\!/_{10}$ d. ${}^{11}\!/_{60}$ f. ${}^1\!/_{295}$
   b. ${}^{11}\!/_{20}$ e. ${}^4\!/_5$ g. ${}^{10}\!/_{177}$
   c. ${}^1\!/_5$

Week 30 (pages 92–94)

MONDAY
1. Answer is correct.
   $321 \times 76 = 24{,}396$
2. 55
3. yes
4. 80°
5. a. $3.90
   b. $5.50
   c. $9.26
   d. $3.90 – $28.60

TUESDAY
1. c, d,
2. Answers will vary.
3. 0.33
4. 76; 640; 700; 206
5. a. 3; b. 12,000 cm; c. 9,000;
   d. 272; e.11; f. 432; g. 30; h. 8

WEDNESDAY
1. The hours of the restaurants are unnecessary. Answer = 192 ft^2
2. –84
3. $q = -6.75$
4. rectangular prism
5. t,t; t,c; t,m; rb,t; rb,c; rb,m; h,t; h,c; h,m; ch,t; ch,c; ch,m

THURSDAY
1. ${}^1\!/_{15}$
2. 97 (The pattern is double the previous number and subtract one.)
3. $5a^2 + 6c^2 + a - 29$
4. August 6
5. a. $2\frac{1}{2}$ in   b. 10 cm

FRIDAY
1. no; correct answer is $48,236.75
2. c, d
3. 9,000
4. c
5. a. $1.47;   b. $1.29;
   c. $30.81;   d. $3.76
   e. $12.91

Week 31 (pages 95–97)

MONDAY
1. Missing info: the number of slices in the loaf of bread
2. 45, R 4
3. ${}^{26}\!/_{51}$
4. Answers will vary; (n, m) = (3, 4) or (6, 8)
5. rectangular prism

TUESDAY
1. 145
2. –5880
3. 18
4. no
5. 72.3 in^3

WEDNESDAY
1. –116
2. Answers will vary depending on date.
3. $12n^7 + 14n^2$
4. Check drawings for accuracy.
5. About 4,200

THURSDAY
1. 2.8
2. ${}^{12}\!/_1$
3. true
4. $n = 3, -3$
5. 527.52 cm^2

FRIDAY
1. division
2. 832
3. $264

4. $y = -15$
5. b

Week 32 (pages 98–100)

MONDAY
1. 2,664,000
2. Dependent events: The outcome of one event affects the outcome of the second event. Independent events: the outcomes of the events are not affected by one another.
3. no
4. 2 faces, 1 edge, 1 vertex
5. a. 800,695
   b. 322,284
   c. 482,423

TUESDAY
1. 4.532
2. 3105
3. $7b - 10a + c - 3$
4. a. 2; b. 1; c. 9; d. 5
5. No (two 500-pound bags would be sufficient).

WEDNESDAY
1. a. true; b. true
2. the sum of nine and four times a number (x) divided by twelve
3. ${}^2\!/_7$
4. $-1{,}650\,x + 4{,}290$
5. Answers will vary. Students may first change the fraction of an hour to minutes.

THURSDAY
1. $1\,{}^9\!/_{20}$
2. 6
3. 60,970,000
4. the cylinder
5. $x + (x - 215) = 563; x = 389$
   (Prof. Zoom went back 389 years.)
   2004 – 389 = year 1615

FRIDAY
1. a
2. 20,000
3. $x = 5$; yes
4. 3,540
5. A. 3 hrs, 13 min
   B. 265
   C. 3:26 p.m.

Week 33 (pages 101–103)

MONDAY
1. 880,000,000
2. 2.356×10^7
3. The answer depends on the value of b.
4. cylinder

5. $^2/_3$

TUESDAY
1. $-q + p = -12$
2. $^1/_9$; $^1/_5$; $^4/_{11}$
3. 370,000,000
4. 0.55
5. Proportion: $^9/_{22} = ^x/_{176}$;
   Answer: 72

WEDNESDAY
1. all are 60°
2. –2,150
3. $c = 4^2/_3$
4. 1,056 ft
5. d

THURSDAY
1. $^5/_{81}$
2. Answers will vary; there are several possibilities. Make sure students' answers total $37.25.
3. 4.2×10^6
4. 1.5899
5. a. miles
   b. years, decades, or centuries
   c. tons, tones, pounds, or kilograms
   d. gallons, cubic feet, cubic meters
   e. liters, cups, quarts, pints, gallons
   f. feet, meters

FRIDAY
1. c
2. yes
3. d
4. 6,170,000
5.

7	9	5	4	8	2	3	1	6
1	6	3	9	5	7	8	4	2
2	4	8	3	1	6	7	9	5
4	1	6	7	2	3	9	5	8
5	7	9	1	4	8	2	6	3
3	8	2	6	9	5	1	7	4
9	3	7	8	6	4	5	2	1
6	2	1	5	3	9	4	8	7
8	5	4	2	7	1	6	3	9

Week 34 (pages 104–106)

MONDAY
1. 114,710
2. $^{19}/_{33}$
3. $2n + 12$
4. the prism
5. 1,635 days

TUESDAY
1. 822.649
2. 64.36 km
3. $b = -1$

4. $^8/_1$
5. 12,250 cm^3

WEDNESDAY
1. 8°
2. $^5/_2$
3. true
4. yes
5. no

THURSDAY
1. $28^{20}/_{21}$
2. 129°
3. 15, –6, 0, –3
4. no
5. 140,000

FRIDAY
1. $8 + (4k + 66)$
2. 1,811.02
3. $98 - b = 13b$
4. 35.25 ft^2
5. 29,000 yards or about $16^1/_2$ miles.

Week 35 (pages 107–109)

MONDAY
1. 48
2. 77
3. $^7/_{34}$
4. Rule: subtract 10, then 20, then 30, then 40, and so on from the previous number; Missing: 1,110; 1,020
5. Check drawings to see that they are symmetrical.

TUESDAY
1. 160.1157
2. none
3. $2,694,640,000
4. 3918.72 cm^2
5. 2^6; 9^2; 6^3; 3^5; 4^4

WEDNESDAY
1. 124,336
2. table
3. $g = -24$
4. Check figures to see that all sides are equal and no angles are right angles.
5. $160,000

THURSDAY
1. $5^1/_{12}$
2. 42.1%
3. five thousand; fifty; five hundredths; five thousandths
4. Subtract 3 from 10.
5. no

FRIDAY
1. 3.5 min
2. e

3. $^{80}/_{91}$
4. yes
5. Answers will vary. Make sure plans total 8,500 seats and have a reasonable arrangement of seats.

Week 36 (pages 110–112)

MONDAY
1. 1250 B.C.
2. 827,115
3. $^8/_{35}$
4. Answers will vary; this could be a rectangular pyramid or a triangular prism.
5. b, d

TUESDAY
1. 208.3
2. five
3. $d = 5, -5$
4. about 1,100 km
5. Answers will vary somewhat. Approximately 58 square units.

WEDNESDAY
1. –29,000
2. d
3. $2f + g$
4. DBE, DBF, DBC
5. Information that is not necessary: Sixty-seven of those interviewed claimed that they believe Atlantis really existed.

THURSDAY
1. 85%
2. $17^{17}/_{18}$
3. 4
4. 132
5. a. 0.179   d. 40
   b. 20,000   e. 0.01 m^3
   c. 5,000,000 mm   f. 8.8 kg

FRIDAY
1. + ; +
2. 24 days
3. 80
4. $9n - (-40)$ OR $- (-40) + 9n$
5.